the merging
of diverse,
distinct,
or separate
elements
into a
unified whole

Suffering Servants

\ 'sə f(ə) riŋ 'sər vənts \ n.:

a theme throughout Scripture

by Chad Bird

CONCORDIA PUBLISHING HOUSE · SAINT LOUIS

Copyright © 2005 Concordia Publishing House
3558 S. Jefferson Ave., St. Louis, MO 63118–3968
1-800-325-3040 • www.cph.org

Written by Chad Bird
Edited by Mark S. Sengele
Designed by Karol Bailey

Unless otherwise indicated, all Scripture quotations are from The Holy Bible, English Standard Version. Copyright © 2001 by Crossways Bibles, a division of Good News Publishers. Used by permission. All rights reserved.

Scripture quotations marked NIV are taken from the HOLY BIBLE, NEW INTERNATIONAL VERSION®. NIV®. Copyright © 1973, 1978, 1984 by International Bible Society. Used by permission of Zondervan Publishing House. All rights reserved.

Scripture quotations marked KJV are from the King James or Authorized Version of the Bible.

Scripture quotations marked NKJV are taken from the New King James Version. Copyright © 1979, 1980, 1982 by Thomas Nelson, Inc. Used by permission. All rights reserved.

Selected Collects from *Lutheran Service Book,* copyright © 2006 Concordia Publishing House. All rights reserved.

Catechism quotations are from *Luther's Small Catechism with Explanation,* copyright © 1986, 1991 Concordia Publishing House. All rights reserved.

Quotations marked AE are from Luther's Works, American Edition: volume 6 copyright © 1970, volume 7 copyright © 1965, and volume 26 copyright © 1963 by Concordia Publishing House; volume 51 copyright © 1959 and volume 52 copyright © 1974 by Fortress Press.

Selected prayers quoted from *Lutheran Book of Prayer,* rev. ed., copyright © 2005 Concordia Publishing House. All rights reserved.

Quote from *An Explanation of the History of the Suffering and Death of Our Lord Jesus Christ* by Johann Gerhard used by permission of Repristination Press.

This publication may be available in braille, in large print, or on cassette tape for the visually impaired. Please allow 8 to 12 weeks for delivery. Write to the Library for the Blind, 7550 Watson Rd., St. Louis, MO 63119-4409; call toll-free 1-888-215-2455; or visit the Web site: www.blindmission.org.

Your comments and suggestions concerning the material are appreciated. Please write the Editor of Youth Materials, Concordia Publishing House, 3558 S. Jefferson Avenue, St. Louis, MO 63118-3968.

Manufactured in the United States of America

1   2   3   4   5   6   7   8   9   10   14   13   12   11   10   09   08   07   06   05

TABLE OF CONTENTS

INTRODUCTION

About the Fusion Series

Fusion—the merging of diverse, distinct, or separate elements into a unified whole. Fusion is a word that speaks of energy and excitement, whether you are talking about a style of music or a nuclear reaction.

God's Word is filled with fusion. The Old Testament bears many hints of events to come in the New Testament, yet we often miss the connection. The *Gospel message* of the Savior is seen time and time again in the Old Testament. Through this series you will come to connect—fuse—those events and messages for yourself and your participants.

Each study in the Fusion Series gathers stories from Scripture—both Old and New Testaments—around a common theme. Through the study of that theme we pray that you come to a deeper understanding of the Gospel message of Jesus Christ as Lord and Savior.

Fusion—Suffering Servants

From the opening pages of the Bible to the end of Revelation, our Lord is there, embracing His creation to such an extent that over and over He takes even its most simple elements and uses them for extraordinary good. In God's Word we meet servants of God whose lives anticipate the suffering of Jesus Christ. Through this study you will meet them too and learn how their lives can impact yours. Most important, in this study you will see your loving Savior whose life, suffering, death, and resurrection assure you of life eternal with Him.

Using These Materials

Fusion Series Bible studies are designed to challenge your participants to develop a deeper knowledge and understanding of Scripture. These studies are designed to work for a large-group presentation or small-group Bible study. While there are six sessions outlined in the book, we have not suggested time limits for each section of the lesson. The level of participant interest, discussion, and further questions will help establish the length of time spent on each section. This flexibility also allows you to use this material for more than six one-hour sessions. You can easily adapt this material to twelve or more hour-long lessons.

Each session contains reproducible participant pages. These pages may be given to participants as you work through the lesson together in class. As an alternative, you may give copies of these pages to participants in advance of the session so that they may complete their personal study before coming to class.

The leader materials work through the questions from the participant pages and provide additional commentary and insights for the Bible class leader. You will want to study these notes as you prepare to lead each session.

It is assumed that the Bible class leader will have the usual basic equipment and supplies available—pencils or pens for each participant and a chalkboard or its equivalent (whiteboard, overhead transparency projector, or newsprint pad and easel) with corresponding markers or chalk. Encourage the participants to bring their own Bibles. Then they can mark useful passages and make notes to guide their personal Bible study and reference later. Do provide additional Bibles, however, for visitors or participants who do not bring one. The appropriate participant pages should be copied in a quantity sufficient for the class.

1

THE DREAMER JOSEPH

Opening Prayer

Almighty God, heavenly Father, who mercifully sustained Joseph in the midst of his trials and temptations, grant unto us, Your servants, that peace which the world cannot give. That as we pass through sufferings, we too may remain faithful to You and Your Word. Through Jesus Christ, our Lord. Amen.

A Dream Come True

Discuss what it means for a person to have his or her dreams come true. Note also that for many people, before their dreams come true, life may be full of ups and downs, so much so that it often feels more like a nightmare coming true.

One might say that Joseph's life was a sort of dream come true, but far from the fairy-tale sense. Joseph's life did indeed unfold according to dreams, but these were not his own dreamlike wishes or desires. Rather, these were God-given, prophetic dreams. These divine dreams eventually "came

true," that is, they came to fulfillment in God's own time and in God's own way.

As they did, however, Joseph's life often seemed more like a nightmare than anything else. He was despised by his brothers, sold into slavery by them while still a teenager, falsely accused by the wife of his master, and finally cast into an Egyptian dungeon. Not exactly a dream life for sure! Joseph seemed to be caught in a whirlpool of suffering that pulled him more and more into the vortex of the grave itself.

In other words, though everything that happened to Joseph was, in reality, his dreams coming true, it seemed exactly the opposite. It appeared as if the God who had given him these dreams had become his enemy. It looked as if the very opposite of what the Lord promised was coming to be. Because of this, Joseph was called to live by faith in the word of promise spoken by God. The Lord who gave him these dreams wanted Joseph to live by the divine Word, not his personal feelings. The Father wanted him to believe the opposite of what he felt and what only appeared to be true.

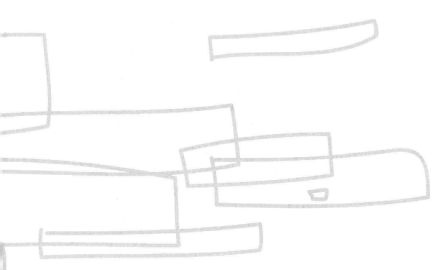

Finally, after a long and drawn-out period of suffering, Joseph was made the right-hand man of Pharaoh. In that office, his dreams did come true. His family—and many others—bowed down to him as the powerful savior who rescued them from famine and death. Though those he loved had intended evil against him, his heavenly Father made everything work out for good, "As for you, you meant evil against me, but God meant it for good, to bring it about that many people should be kept alive, as they are today" (Genesis 50:20). God promises the same for all His children: "And we know that for those who love God all things work together for good, for those who are called according to His purpose" (Romans 8:28).

Joseph was one of many "suffering servants" we read about in the words of the Scriptures. In his life, we see a foreshadowing of what the Suffering Servant—Jesus Christ—would endure for the life of the world. Our heavenly Father provided in Joseph a blueprint, as it were, for the sufferings and eventual glorification of His Son. By placing the lives of Joseph and Jesus side by side, we can better understand what happened to both of them. We can also better understand the way in which God works in our own lives, especially during times of loss, pain, and suffering. As He did for Joseph and as He did for our Lord Jesus, our loving Father will eventually raise us from suffering and death to life in Him.

One Big Unhappy Family

If we had a portrait of Joseph's family, there would probably be very few smiles on their faces. More likely, we'd see brothers scowling at brothers, wives casting jealous glances at one another, and daddy Jacob caught in the middle, looking like a man trapped in a domestic war zone. Yes, indeed, the family into which Joseph was born was not exactly full of happiness and contentment—quite the opposite!

Briefly survey the history of Jacob in Genesis 29–36. How many women did he marry, and how many women bore children for him? Who were his favorites and why? What kind of family problems did such favoritism lead to?

How, in general, would you characterize Jacob's family life?

Read Genesis 37:1–11. Who was the mother of Joseph? In what way did this influence his relationship with his father, Jacob?

It all began when Jacob slipped wedding rings on the fingers of two sisters, Leah and Rachel, who were thereafter in a constant tug-of-war over the heart of their husband. It was a sort of love triangle, but of the isosceles sort—an unequal triangle, with the line between Jacob and Rachel being the shortest. Each wife wanted to conceive more sons for Jacob than the other. So desperate was their competition that they even let their husband have intercourse with their maidservants, Bilhah and Zilpah, who served as surrogate mothers for them! All together, these four women gave birth to a dozen sons.

Leah was the mother of Reuben, Simeon, Levi, Judah, Issachar, and Zebulum. Leah's servant, Zilpah, gave birth to Gad and Asher. Rachel's servant, Bilhah, bore Dan and Naphtali. Rachel was the mother of Joseph and Benjamin.

As a husband, Jacob did not always love his wives equally. So also, he did not love all his sons equally. Because Jacob had always been more devoted to Rachel than to Leah, he loved her sons—Joseph and Benjamin—more than the children of the other mothers. Such conditions certainly were not the ingredients for a story that would end "happily ever after"!

What was the relationship between Joseph and his brothers? What factors led to this relationship?

If the situation in this family weren't complicated enough, when Joseph was in his late teens, three things happened that would cast a very dark shadow over the family for years to come. First, Joseph, who had been pasturing the flock with his brothers, brought back a "bad report" about them (Genesis 37:2). What this "report" consisted of is not explained. But it certainly did not make the brothers happy to have their little brother tattling on

them! Second, we are told that Jacob loved Joseph more than his other sons and thus made him a "coat of many colors" (Genesis 37:3 KJV). When the brothers saw this jacket, the only color they saw was red! This present, of course, made even more visible the father's preference for Joseph. Though intended as a gift of love, for the brothers this coat became a symbol of their own hatred for their brother. "But when his brothers saw that their father loved him [Joseph] more than all his brothers, they hated him and could not speak peacefully to him" (Genesis 37:4).

Summarize the two dreams of Joseph. What was their interpretation? Contrast the true meaning and intent of these dreams with the brothers' reaction. What were they reacting against? How should they have reacted? Was Joseph wrong to tell his family about these dreams? Why or why not? As you answer these questions, consider whether one could call these dreams the Word of God to Joseph. How is Joseph like a preacher?

The most significant events were the dual dreams Joseph had about this time (Genesis 37:5–11). In the first dream, Joseph and his brothers were binding sheaves in the field. His sheaf stood upright, while those of his brothers gathered around and bowed down to the sheaf of Joseph. When Joseph relayed this dream to his brothers, they instantly saw what it symbolized: that Joseph would rule over them. The next dream was similar: the sun, moon, and stars were bowing down to Joseph. Joseph told this dream to his brothers and his father. This troubled even Jacob, who took his son to task: "What is this dream that you have dreamed? Shall I and your mother and your brothers indeed come to bow ourselves to the ground before you?" (Genesis 37:10). The message of the dream was crystal clear. Sometime in the future, God would exalt Joseph to such a degree that he would be supreme over the rest of his family, his parents included. The response of his brothers was also clear: "They hated him [Joseph] even more for his dreams and for his words" (Genesis 37:8).

All too often, one hears Joseph described as a

sort of spoiled brat who took advantage of his father's love to rub these dreams—like salt—into the wounded hearts of his brothers. But nothing could be more unfounded. There is absolutely no evidence in the story itself (or anywhere else in the Bible) that Joseph acted from evil, selfish motives. In fact, the Scriptures have not a single negative word to say about him. Since Joseph truly believed these dreams came from God, and thus that they revealed the will of the Lord for his family, why should he not relay them to his father and brothers? They were prophetic dreams; they foretold what would be. Therefore, in fact, Joseph would have acted wrongly had he not made them known to his family! He was obligated to act as a sort of preacher who proclaimed what God revealed to him. He could not control the response of his family. A preacher never can. He is only called to make known the will of the Lord—whether that will is loved or hated, believed or disbelieved.

Jesus, too, was promised that He would be exalted above others. He also was hated because of this. In what way can we say this hatred was actually hatred for God's Word?

We begin here to see how what happened to this suffering servant of God parallels to some extent what happened to the Suffering Servant, Jesus Christ. The hatred felt and shown toward both of them was in reality hatred of the Word of God itself. Our heavenly Father entrusted both Joseph and Jesus with the sacred task of making known His Word—a Word that was not welcome news to many who heard it. Indeed, this good Word was misinterpreted by them as the exact opposite—a declaration of war! The message Jesus preached and the dreams Joseph preached both proclaimed that the preacher would one day be exalted above those around him.

In both cases, however, this exaltation was twisted by those who heard of it as prideful self-exaltation. But it was a divine gift for others, not self-promotion! Our Lord Jesus was exalted not for His own good but for the good of us sinners that He might give salvation to us. Similarly, Joseph was exalted in Egypt not for his own good, but for the good of his family, the Egyptians, and people everywhere who were in danger of dying from hunger. Also, through Joseph, the family given the promise of the Messiah—his own family—was able to survive and pass on that promise. But as the brothers of Joseph did not understand nor give thanks to God for these divine dreams, so the people around Jesus misunderstood His message and hated Him for it.

Thanks be to God, however, that despite opposition from sinners, He still brings His Word to fulfillment. Indeed, despite the fact that sinners often hate the very message that is given to save them, God remains faithful. He does what He says. He brings us to repentance. And, in hindsight, we see the good that God intended for us, despite the evil we intended against Him and His messengers.

Betrayed and Sold

Read Genesis 37:12–36. When Joseph is seen by his brothers, what is their reaction? Earlier we read that Joseph was "hated" by his brothers (37:4). Read Matthew 5:21–26 and 1 John 3:11–15. What commandment is related to hatred? Why are they so closely related? Consider the action of Joseph's brothers. What did their hatred lead to?

Hatred is rarely content to remain inside a person. Whether in word or deed, it eventually explodes, often with the ferocity and deadliness of an erupting volcano. In the New Testament, Matthew declares that he who hates has already sinned against the Fifth Commandment. John reminds his readers of the slippery slope into murderous hatred demonstrated by Cain. So it was with the brothers of Joseph. They eventually saw their chance to seek revenge against the one whom their father favored: the "dreamer." And the lava of hatred spewed forth.

What was the initial plan of the brothers? What did Judah convince them to do instead? In what way would this second plan benefit the brothers even more?

The chance came when their father, Jacob, sent

Joseph to check on his brothers, who were pasturing the flock some distance away from home. After a dead end or two, Joseph found out where his brothers were camped. The biblical story is quite blunt about their reaction:

> They saw [Joseph] from afar, and before he came near to them they conspired against him to kill him. They said to one another, "Here comes this dreamer. Come now, let us kill him and throw him into one of the pits. Then we will say that a fierce animal has devoured him, and we will see what will become of his dreams." (Genesis 37:18–20)

Their plan is as simple as it is sinister. Hatred conceives murder, and murder gives birth to lies. Such is the nature of sin. It is never satiated; the word *enough* is not in its vocabulary. All sin wants is more, more, and still more.

But sin is not greater than God, who intervenes here for Joseph, as He also intervened many times for His own Son before the appointed time of Jesus' crucifixion. One of the brothers, Reuben, serves as the Lord's instrument of redemption. He did not want Joseph dead. In fact, he wanted to restore him to his father but knew that to do so he would have to play his cards right. So he suggested the brothers not kill Joseph but only cast him into a pit, thus allowing Reuben time to hatch a plan to rescue his brother (Genesis 37:22). Reuben's idea worked, at least in part. They did not murder their brother. Instead, they ripped off Joseph's much-hated "coat of many colors," threw him into the waterless pit, and—as if to prove their callousness—sat down beside their brother's earthen prison to eat a meal.

About this time, a caravan of foreigners happened by, on their way down to Egypt. One of the brothers, Judah, began seeing dollar signs. He said, "What profit is it if we kill our brother and conceal his blood? Come, let us sell him to the Ishmaelites, and let not our hand be upon him, for he is our brother, our own flesh" (Genesis 37:26–27). Once more, the other brothers (except Reuben) consented, up was lifted Joseph, and into the hands of the traders he was sold—sold into shackles for twenty shekels of silver. One can almost hear the brothers cackling as their little brother is led away in chains, "Ha! Now let's see the dreams of Daddy's favorite come true!"

After getting their revenge against Joseph, how did they seek to get revenge against their father?

One might think the brothers' vengeful scheme was wrapped up now, but the final blow was about to be struck, and it would land right on the heart of their father. Taking Joseph's coat, they dipped it in the blood of a goat, then handed it over to their father with these heartless words, "This we have found; please identify whether it is your son's robe or not" (Genesis 37:32). Great was the grief that gripped Jacob's soul! The coat that once meant, "You are my beloved son," had come to mean, "My beloved son is dead!" Jacob's heart shattered. He refused the comfort—both real and feigned—extended to him by his sons and daughters. Weeping, he lamented, "No, I shall go down to Sheol to my son, mourning" (Genesis 37:35).

Relate these events to Joseph's dreams. How did all this teach Joseph to live by and believe in the Word of God? Read Hebrews 11:1 and relate it to Joseph.

Read Psalm 105:17–19. How do these verses describe Joseph? What was the Lord doing to Joseph?

The sufferings of both Jacob and Joseph are a vivid reminder that God's ways are not man's ways. God does not hesitate to place heavy crosses on the shoulders of those whom He loves. For years to come, Jacob will grieve over the "death" of his beloved son. Likewise, Joseph will live apart from his family, in slavery, and finally be thrown into a dungeon. Life will be a bed of thorns, not roses. But through every dark and dismal day, the Lord of light never forsakes them. That is God's way. He gives strength to the weak, hope to the downtrodden, life to the dead. The word of promise He gave to Joseph in dreams, and through Joseph to his brothers and father—that word would come to pass. It will be years in coming, to be sure. But such is the life of faith. It lives by that which is unseen. For "faith is the assurance of things hoped for, the conviction of things not seen" (Hebrews 11:1). This life of faith was a time of testing for Joseph. The Lord was preparing him for the tasks ahead. Thus, as the psalmist reflected upon the life of Joseph, he sang,

> He had sent a man ahead of them, Joseph, who was sold as a slave. His feet were hurt with fetters; his neck was put in a collar of iron; until what he had said came to pass, the word of the LORD tested him. (Psalm 105:17–19)

Thanks be to God!—Joseph passed that test.

Martin Luther calls Joseph an "image of God's Son." In what ways do the sufferings of Joseph parallel the sufferings in the life of Jesus?

As Martin Luther reflected upon the sufferings of Jacob and Joseph, he also saw revealed here the pattern that would be repeated and superceded in the sufferings of God's Son. In answer to the question of why God allows men to make such cruel crosses for others, as Joseph's brothers made for him and Jacob, Luther responds,

> My reply is that God wants us to consider and learn how great the love of parents towards children is, that we may estimate from this the magnitude of God's love by which He embraced us when He was willing to let His only-begotten Son suffer and be crucified for us. For Joseph is the image of God's Son. (AE 6:384–85)

In other words, Jacob's love for Joseph is like the love of our heavenly Father, only God's love is infinitely greater. Jacob loved Joseph much, but God loves us even more—so much that He was willing to send His only-begotten Son to suffer and die for us. Thus in the love of Jacob we see revealed, in a small but significant way, the love of our heavenly Father for us.

Moreover, in Joseph we see "the image of God's Son," as Luther says. What does this "image" mean? It means that God arranges Joseph's life so that it is a kind of preview of what Jesus would do and suffer for our salvation. As it was with Joseph, so it will be with Jesus to a much greater extent. Luther speaks elsewhere about how

all the stories in the Scriptures—including these about Joseph—are to be read through the prism of Christ.

> For this reason, too, all the narratives of the Old Testament point so nicely and beautifully to Christ and confess Him; all of them, indeed, stand around Him, just as Anna physically stood in his presence [at the temple]. It affords great pleasure to read and hear how they all look and point toward Christ . . . [Here is an] example: Joseph was sold into Egypt and became a ruler over the country after his imprisonment. This happened and was written that he might prefigure Christ, who became through his passion Lord of all the world. Who has time enough to explain all these stories and to see how Samson, David, Solomon, Aaron, and others literally and accurately signify Christ? (AE 52:126).

Of course, Luther here is only echoing what Jesus Himself often stated. For instance, He says to the Jews, "You search the Scriptures because you think that in them you have eternal life; and it is they that bear witness about Me. . . . If you believed Moses, you would believe Me, for he wrote of Me" (John 5:39, 46). Or, during His walk with the Emmaus disciples, "beginning with [the five books of] Moses and all the [writings of the] Prophets, [Jesus] interpreted to them in all the Scriptures the things concerning Himself" (Luke 24:27). Let us therefore ask in what way this story about Joseph being betrayed by his brothers, cast in the pit, and sold into slavery—let us ask what all this suffering has to do with Jesus? Or, as we inquired earlier, "In what way is Joseph 'the image of God's Son'?"

Read John 1:11; 7:5; and 15:18. Compare this to Joseph. Read Matthew 26:15. How is this similar to what happened to Joseph?

Consider, first of all, the hatred of the brothers and their plotting against Joseph. His own flesh and blood did not receive him. Instead, they despised him because he was the beloved of his father, the chosen son, the one whom God would exalt over them. Therefore, they plotted and carried out evil against him. So it was also with the Lord Jesus. He came down from heaven to take on our own flesh and blood. He became part of the human family. As the evangelist John writes, "He came to His own, and His own people did not receive Him" (John 1:11). Instead, the sinful world hated this chosen Son who was beloved by His Father (John 15:18). Indeed, "not even His brothers believed in Him" (John 7:5). Rather than receiving Jesus as the one chosen by the Father, they plotted and carried out evil against Him.

For Joseph, this evil took the form of being seized, cast into a pit, and sold into slavery for twenty shekels of silver. Here, too, we observe the parallels between the sufferings of Joseph and Jesus. Our Lord was seized and arrested by those to whom He was sent by the Father. On the night in which Christ was betrayed, He went to the Garden of Gethsemane. There the soldiers, led by Judas Iscariot, took Him into custody and placed Him in chains.

Joseph was sold into the hands of the Gentiles—the Ishmaelites/Midianites—by His brothers for a mere twenty shekels of silver. Jesus, too, was sold into the hands of the Gentiles—the Romans—by one of His own disciples, Judas, for thirty pieces of silver (Matthew 26:15). In connection with this, Luther explains this as one of the ways in which Joseph is an "image of God's Son." He comments:

> Joseph was sold for a smaller price than Christ was, and I think that the price was about 20 thalers. I am not inclined to engage in rather minute discussions on silver coins. But from this passage [Genesis 37:28] Zechariah undoubtedly derived his prophecy concerning Christ (Zechariah 11:12): "They weighed out as my wages thirty shekels of silver." For facts and circumstances agree excellently, and there cannot be a greater similarity than that between Christ crucified and Joseph; the selling and death of both are in agreement. For as Isaiah (53:8) says of Christ, "He was cut off out of the land of the living," so also Joseph is removed from the land and sight of his father, just as if he would never return to his father or see him again. (AE 6:391–92)

Thus both Joseph and Jesus were handed over by those close to them—brothers and a disciple—for what amounted to a handful of dollars.

Closing Prayer

Lord Jesus, King of kings, today again I praise You with my hosannas and welcome You as the King of my heart. Enter in and take full possession of me, body, heart, mind, and soul. As thousands and ten thousands today vow faithfulness to You until death, acknowledging that they have no other Savior, grant that I, too, join this great host of faithful people to realize both the enormity and bitterness of my sin as well as the course of plenteous redemption to which You committed Yourself.

I confess, gracious Savior, that I have not been true to You as You have been to me. Other interests have placed themselves above You in my thoughts. Have mercy on me, and forgive me my transgressions. Sprinkle me with Your blood and wash me clean from the stain of my sin. Strengthen my heart with the assurance of my adoption and transform me according to Your image by the daily renewing of my Baptism. Preserve me in faith until the end of days, that I may behold You in glory evermore. Hear my cry King of my heart and Savior of my soul. Amen.

(Prayer for Palm Sunday, *Lutheran Book of Prayer*, p. 128)

THE DREAMER JOSEPH

A Dream Come True

Discuss what it means for a person to have his or her dreams come true. Note also that for many people, before their dreams come true, life may be full of ups and downs, so much so that it often feels more like a nightmare coming true.

One Big Unhappy Family

Briefly survey the history of Jacob in **Genesis 29–36**. How many women did he marry, and how many women bore children for him? Who were his favorites and why? What kind of family problems did such favoritism lead to? How, in general, would you characterize Jacob's family life?

Read **Genesis 37:1–11**. Who was the mother of Joseph? In what way did this influence his relationship with his father, Jacob?

What was the relationship between Joseph and his brothers? What factors led to this relationship?

Summarize the two dreams of Joseph. What was their interpretation? Contrast the true meaning and intent of these dreams with the brothers' reaction. What were they reacting against? How should they have reacted?

Was Joseph wrong to tell his family about these dreams? Why or why not? As you answer these questions, consider whether one could call these dreams the word of God to Joseph. How is Joseph like a preacher?

Jesus, too, was promised that He would be exalted above others. He also was hated because of this. In what way can we say this hatred was actually hatred for God's Word?

Betrayed and Sold

Read **Genesis 37:12–36**. When Joseph is seen by his brothers, what is their reaction? Earlier we read that Joseph was "hated" by his brothers (**37:4**). Read **Matthew 5:21–26** and **1 John 3:11–15**. What commandment is related to hatred? Why are they so closely related? Consider the action of Joseph's brothers. What did their hatred lead to?

What was the initial plan of the brothers? What did Judah convince them to do instead? In what way would this second plan benefit the brothers even more?

After getting their revenge against Joseph, how did they seek to get revenge against their father?

Relate these events to Joseph's dreams. How did all this teach Joseph to live by and believe in the Word of God? Read **Hebrews 11:1** and relate it to Joseph.

Read **Psalm 105:17–19**. How do these verses describe Joseph? What was the Lord doing to Joseph?

Martin Luther calls Joseph an "image of God's Son." In what ways do the sufferings of Joseph parallel the sufferings in the life of Jesus?

Read **John 1:11**; **7:5**; and **15:18**. Compare this to Joseph.

Read **Matthew 26:15**. How is this similar to what happened to Joseph?

Read **Zechariah 9:9–11**. Reference to such a "waterless pit" (**v. 11**) occurs only here and in **Genesis 37:24**. Who is released from this pit in Zechariah? Compare this to what happened to Joseph.

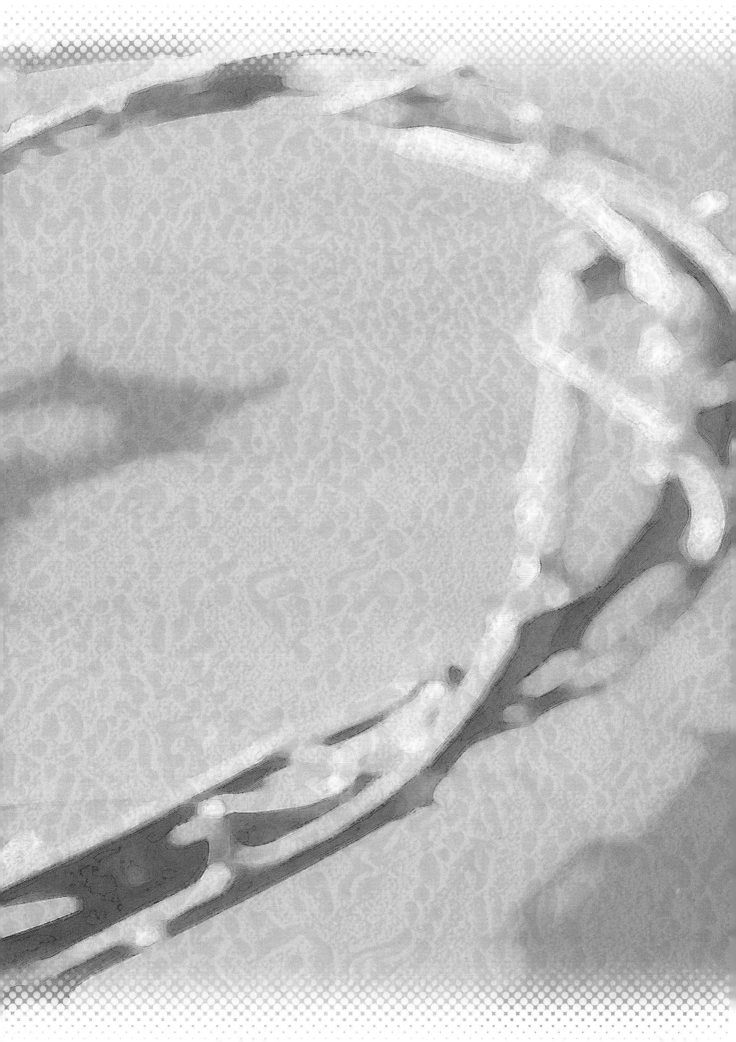

2

INSIDE EGYPT
JOSEPH

Opening Prayer

Lord Jesus, I believe. Help my unbelief! Strengthen my weak and flickering faith. I know that You are my wisdom, my righteousness, my sanctification, and my redemption. Lord, strengthen this faith in me, that I may never fear nor faint in any trial or temptation. You alone are the Author and Finisher of my faith. Though my faith be tried with fire, may I ever be found strong and unmovable to the glory of Your holy name. Let me firmly trust in Your blood, which cleanses me from all sin, that though my sins are as scarlet, they shall be as white as snow. When I am enticed by sin and the world beckons and my own passions want to yield, help my unbelief, and give me the strength and will to resist. When trials, sorrow, and affliction want to rob me of this trust, O Lord, help me to remain steadfast and true. Strengthen my faith in Your promise that all things work together for good to them that love God, to them that are called according to Your purpose to be Your own here in time and there in eternity. You, O almighty Lord, can help; You, O gracious Lord, will help my unbelief; You, O merciful Lord, will strengthen my faith. Lord, I believe! Amen.

(Prayer for Stronger Faith, *Lutheran Book of Prayer,* pp. 182–83)

Spend a few minutes reviewing the events of Joseph's life from the previous lesson. When we left Joseph, his brothers had just sold him to the Ishmaelite/Midianite traders for twenty pieces of silver.

Falsely Accused

Describe Joseph's situation in Egypt. What happened to him once he arrived? Contrast his life in Egypt under Potiphar with what his life had been like while still at home. What kinds of temptations might he have faced in Egypt: doubt, despair, loneliness?

Down went Joseph, a chained slave, to the country of Egypt. How the tears must have flowed as he left behind everything and everyone he knew! Years later, when his brothers recalled the day they sold Joseph, they said to one another, "We saw the distress of his soul, when he begged us and we did not listen" (Genesis 42:21). One might have thought his troubles would soon come to an end. But, as Luther remarks, "Joseph dies in many ways" (AE 6:386) and these "many ways" of dying were just

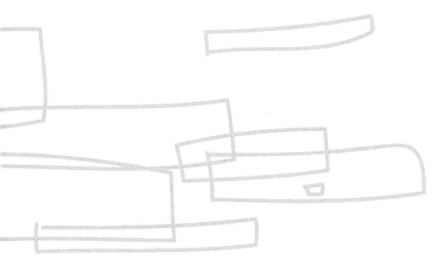

getting started. One might say this young man was undergoing a slow and painful crucifixion as he bore the many crosses placed upon him.

What kind of servant was Joseph? What did his master think of him? What does this reveal about Joseph and the attitude he adopted regarding his new situation? What does this reveal about his hope and his faith?

When the Midianite traders who had purchased Joseph arrived in Egypt, they in turn sold him to a man named Potiphar, an officer of Pharaoh and the captain of the guard. Though still a slave, Joseph was far from being a broken young man. He still had hope, for he still had God. Joseph lived by faith in the words his heavenly Father had spoken to him in his dreams. This prophetic word kept him afloat in his sea of suffering. Indeed, even in captivity, Joseph actually thrived. As Moses writes,

The LORD was with Joseph, and he became a successful man, and he was in the house of his Egyptian master. His master saw that the LORD was with him and that the LORD caused all that he did to succeed in his hands. So Joseph found

favor in his sight and attended him, and he made him overseer of his house and put him in charge of all that he had. (Genesis 39:2–4)

It appeared as if everything was finally going well for Joseph. He was safe, well taken care of, appreciated, industrious, and no doubt admired by his fellow workers and members of the household.

How did Satan use the wife of Potiphar to tempt Joseph? What does this show us about the way the devil works? What would have been Satan's ultimate goal?

How did Joseph respond to her repeated advances? Analyze his response. What reasons does Joseph give for refusing her? What else could Joseph have said? What eventually happens with Potiphar's wife? How was Joseph "rewarded" for his faithful service?

However, just when it seemed everything was brightening up for Joseph, dark clouds appeared on the horizon. We are told Joseph was a good-looking young man (Genesis 39:6). His charming face soon caught the eye of Potiphar's wife. She began to lust after Joseph in her heart, finally propositioning him with her lips. "Come to bed with me!" (Genesis 39:7 NIV), she said seductively. Not once, not twice, but daily she tried to lure him into having sex with her (Genesis 39:10). All of her adulterous invitations, however, were met by Joseph's steadfast NO! He told "Mrs. Potiphar" that, in essence, his master—her husband—had held back nothing from him except one thing—her. Therefore, he concluded, "How then can I do this great wickedness and sin against God" (Genesis 39:9). No matter how great the temptation, he would not sew the "scarlet letter" onto his life, nor did he wish that stigma attached to her.

But Joseph's refusals did little to quench Mrs. Pothiphar's flames of lust. The day came when all the men who served in Potiphar's house were out and about, and the boss's wife caught Joseph alone. She seized the opportunity . . . and Joseph's clothes as well! "Come to bed with me!" (39:12 NIV), she lured once more. Yet again, Joseph refused—though not so much with words as with actions. He high-tailed it out of the house, but in his hasty exit he left his outer garment in the grasping hands of Potiphar's wife.

In this action, Scripture seems to back up the old saying "Hell hath no fury like a woman scorned." This wife's adulterous advances had been rejected one too many times, so her hunger of lust gave way to a thirst for revenge. Using Joseph's garment as "evidence" against him, Potiphar's wife raised a cry that this Hebrew servant tried to rape her but fled when she resisted and screamed. She later repeated the same bogus story to her husband. He, of course, believed her lie, was enraged at Joseph, and threw his servant behind bars in the place where the king's prisoners where confined. There sat poor Joseph, unjustly accused, innocently imprisoned, suffering once more under the cross of death.

Compare this incident in the life of Joseph with the various false accusations leveled against Jesus. In what ways were both men faithful to the task given them by God? What kinds of accusations were leveled against Jesus? See Matthew 9:34; 11:19; 26:65; and 27:29. How did both of these men react?

Where was God when both Joseph and Jesus were suffering? Why does God allow such sufferings to befall His servants? How does God use pain, grief, and loss in our lives in a similar way?

Is not the plight of Joseph also that of Jesus? Compare their lives. For several years, Joseph labored faithfully in the house of Potiphar. The Lord was with him and blessed him in all he did. Time and again he resisted the sexual temptations thrown at him by his master's wife. Yet in the end, how do men reward him for his good and faithful service? With nothing but betrayal, lies, dishonor, and imprisonment. No doubt his enemies even accused him of using his good record as nothing but a cloak behind which to hide his scheme to rape the master's wife.

So it was also in the life of Jesus. Never was a man more faithful in His service to God and His fellow man than was our Lord. All He did was good and right. Every temptation thrown at Him was resisted. Yet over and over, His enemies—as well as His friends—betrayed Him. When He demonstrated love by casting demons out of people, His adversaries claimed this was nothing but a cloak behind which to hide His devotion to the devil. "He casts out demons by the prince of demons," the Pharisees slandered (Matthew 9:34). He is maligned as a glutton and drunkard (Matthew 11:19). He is accused of blaspheming God (Matthew 26:65). Soldiers mock Him as a fake king (Matthew 27:29). All this vilification and these trumped-up charges come from the very people whom Jesus was sent to serve! They are like Potiphar's wife—ungrateful and hateful. They desire nothing more than punishment for the One who would not do and would not be what they so wickedly wanted Him to do and be. Joseph ended up being "crucified" in prison, while Jesus suffered on His very real cross.

Where is God in all this suffering of His servants? Right there with them, that's where. He is faithful. He is compassionate. His ways are not man's ways. He did not send Jesus down from heaven to lead a life of ease on the shores of the Sea of Galilee. He sent Him to suffer and die, to bear the sins, accusations, and hatred of the world—our sins, our accusations, and, yes, our hatred. Glorification came only after the cross—so also with Joseph. The Lord sent him down to Egypt to save many people, but first came the suffering and the cross. Joseph had many deaths he needed to die before being promoted to Pharaoh's right hand. In all this, Joseph was like a mini-Jesus, mapping out for us beforehand what the life of Jesus would look like.

Interpreting in Prison . . . and Being Forgotten

What seems to have happened to Joseph's life? As he reflected upon the dreams he had while still with his father, what kinds of thoughts would the devil have planted in his mind? Read Hebrews 11:1. Apply these words to Joseph's situation. What did it mean for him, in his particular situation, to live by faith?

Down, down, down Joseph has fallen. First he was hated, betrayed, and sold by his brothers. Then he was resold by the Midianite traders. His faithful service to Potiphar was rewarded with lying accusations and unjust imprisonment. When would it all stop? How much more could he take? Would he lose faith in God behind bars and finally give up hope that his dreams would ever come true?

No, he would not! Joseph knew that God cannot lie. Our heavenly Father always stands beside those who are His, and He always, always keeps His word. Though all of life virtually screamed, *"GOD HAS REJECTED YOU, JOSEPH!"* he turned a deaf ear to that tempting lie and listened instead to the steady voice of his Father in heaven who promised, "Never will I leave you. Never will I forsake you. At the appropriate time, your dreams will come true."

Compare Joseph's service in Potiphar's house with his service in prison. How are they similar? How did Joseph fare in prison?

Thus, even in prison, Joseph did not wallow in self-pity. Nor did He twiddle his thumbs. He remained active. As when he was serving his father, Jacob, and as when he was working in Potiphar's house, so also in the king's dungeon it soon became evident that the Lord was with Joseph and would bless him in whatever he did. As Moses writes:

The LORD was with Joseph and showed him steadfast love and gave him favor in the sight of the keeper of the prison. And the keeper of the prison put Joseph in charge of all the prisoners who were in the prison. Whatever was done there, he was the one who did it. The keeper of the prison paid no attention to anything that was in Joseph's charge, because the LORD was with him. And whatever he did, the LORD made it succeed. (Genesis 39:21–23)

If these words sound strikingly familiar they should; they echo closely Potiphar's observation regarding Joseph and his faithful service (Genesis 39:2–6).

Summarize what the baker and cupbearer dreamed. Read Genesis 40:8. What is Joseph claiming? If all interpretations belong to God, how could Joseph promise to interpret the dreams? What does this tell us about the way Joseph viewed his relationship with God? How was Joseph the spokesman for the Lord?

During Joseph's incarceration, his life was once more affected by dreams—though this time they were the dreams of others. Two chief servants of Pharaoh landed behind bars: the cupbearer and the baker. One night, both of them had dreams. The next morning, when Joseph saw them, he asked why they had such long faces. "We have had dreams, and there is no one to interpret them," they replied (Genesis 40:8). Joseph responded, "Do not interpretations belong to God? Please tell them to me" (Genesis 40:8). And so they did. The details of the dreams need not detain us. You can read about them in Genesis 40:9–19. Joseph listened and interpreted both in turn. The meaning of the dream of the cupbearer was, essentially, that in three days Pharaoh would "lift up [his] head" to restore him to his office. The meaning of the baker's dream was that, likewise, in three days Pharaoh would "lift up [his] head" . . . but by hanging him from a tree! And so it came to pass, just as Joseph had said. Three days later—on Pharaoh's birthday no less—the cupbearer was once again in the king's service, while the baker's neck was slipped into a noose (Genesis 40:20–23).

Read Genesis 40:14–15. What is Joseph's request? Is he justified in making this request? Why or why not?

We want to highlight the request Joseph made to the cupbearer after he interpreted his dream favorably. He pleaded, "Only remember me, when it is well with you, and please do me the kindness to mention me to Pharaoh, and so get me out of this house. For I was indeed stolen out of the land of the Hebrews, and here also I have done nothing that they should put me into the pit" (Genesis 40:14–15).

Joseph was quite justified, of course, in making this request. If he could somehow gain his freedom—a freedom rightly deserved—through the influence of the chief cupbearer, then by all means he should. He may very well have thought, *"Ah! Finally, God has provided this opportunity for me to leave this undeserved imprisonment!"* As he saw the cupbearer walk free, he saw his own ticket to freedom as well.

The cupbearer is seemingly the only one who could act to have Joseph released, yet what does he do (40:23)? Reading ahead, note for how long the cupbearer kept silent about what Joseph had done for him (41:1)? Put yourself in Joseph's shoes: What would this period of waiting have been like for him?

In what ways is the forgetfulness of the cupbearer typical of sinful humans? How do we treat those who have done good things for us? How do we oftentimes shirk our responsibilities to help others, even if they have formerly assisted us?

Once more, what kind of temptations would have faced Joseph in this situation?

However, the last verse of Genesis 40 falls like a hammer on Joseph's hope, seemingly shattering it. "Yet the chief cupbearer did not remember Joseph, but forgot him" (Genesis 40:23). *Forgot him?! Forgot the man who had raised his spirits when in prison? Forgot the man who had so graciously answered his request for an interpretation? Forgot innocent, faithful Joseph?* Yes. In fact, the cupbearer forgot him, as the story goes on to say, not for a few months or a year, but for two whole years (Genesis 41:1).

Here we see a premier example of the depth of human ingratitude. Oh, indeed, the servant probably had good intentions at first. *"I'll bring up Joseph's situation the first chance I get,"* he may have promised himself. So the first week goes by. Of course, right then, having just been released, he wants to stay on his master's good side, so no need to bring up a subject as touchy as prison just yet. Then two weeks speed by, then three, four, and a few more. The cupbearer grows accustomed to life in the royal court once again. The shame and pain associated with his imprisonment have begun to subside. Any gratitude the cupbearer had for Joseph begins to shrink as well. His claim of innocence seems less and less credible anyway. Finally, after several months, it becomes quite easy to go days without giving any thought to Joseph at all. Alas, such is the human condition—the condition of us all. What we shout for joy over today leaves us yawning six months down the road.

Luther writes: "The very saintly and good Joseph was crucified, died, was buried, and descended into hell during these two years" (AE 7:129). Luther is obviously not speaking literally but is comparing the sufferings of Joseph and Jesus. In what ways are they similar? How can we speak of this time as a "crucifixion" for Joseph? Read Matthew 27:46. What does this cry of Jesus mean? How might Joseph have prayed similarly?

For Joseph, these next two years must have been extremely painful. His hopes were probably high at first. Several weeks go by—nothing happens. Then several months—still nothing. The man whom he helped, seemingly his only means of release from the awful pit, evidently forgot him. The demons surely jumped at this chance to tempt Joseph to despair like they had never done before. *"Look what kind of God you have! He's left you in this hellhole to rot. Is this the God you claim is so good and gracious? He must have forgotten you too. Get real, Joseph. God's the cat, and you're the mouse."* Such were the tortuous thoughts that must have plagued Joseph as he languished through those two years. They attack every saint who suffers through something that feels like divine abandonment.

One is here reminded of Jesus' lamentation from the cross, "My God, My God, why have You forsaken Me?" (Matthew 27:46). Though the words of our Lord reveal infinitely greater pain and sorrow than what Joseph suffered, the same temptation faced them both: to throw away faith and hope. For being fully a man (as well as fully God), Jesus, too, had faith in His heavenly Father. He was a believer, a perfect believer. In fact, in Psalm 22, Jesus goes on to pray, "You [O God] are He who took Me from the womb; You made Me trust You at My mother's breasts" (Psalm 22:9). Jesus trusted in His heavenly Father, yet that trust was assaulted by Satan time and again. What an attack must have been mounted against Him as He hung nailed to the wood, feeling every flame of divine wrath, knowing that the Father has forsaken Him since Jesus had become sin itself (2 Corinthians 5:21). Indeed, you can hear the devilish accents in the words hurled by the taunting crowd of onlookers at the site of the crucifixion:

You who would destroy the temple and rebuild it in three days, save Yourself! If You are the Son of God, come down from the cross. . . . He saved others; He cannot save Himself. He is the King of Israel; let Him come down now from the cross, and we will believe in Him. He trusts in God; let God deliver Him now, if He desires Him. For He said, "I am the Son of God." (Matthew 27:40–43)

Those who uttered these words served as Satan's mouthpiece. Every bitter word was aimed as an arrow at Jesus' heart of faith. Yet none struck home. Christ remained faithful. He did not let doubt drive Him from His Father, off the cross, and into the devil's trap. And all this He did for us.

The two years in which Joseph languished in prison were a kind of prolonged crucifixion. Indeed, Martin Luther reflected upon this painful period of Joseph's life and wrote, "And so the very saintly and good Joseph was crucified, died, was buried, and descended into hell during these two years" (AE 7:129).

Once again, we see what Luther meant when he described Joseph as an "image of God's Son." Joseph is a suffering servant in whose trials and tribulations we behold a blueprint for what will happen to the Suffering Servant, our Lord Jesus. Joseph, too, was sorely tried, but he did not lose faith. The Lord sustained him, as He does all His servants who trust in Him. Though He brings them, at times, down to the lowest pit—even a dungeon!— He brings them back up again. As Hannah once sang, "The LORD kills and brings to life; He brings down to Sheol and raises up" (1 Samuel 2:6). Indeed, we are about to see how Joseph is "resurrected." Luther continues:

Now the Lord will come and will liberate, glorify, and magnify him, just as He called, justified, and gave the Holy Spirit and His Son, who went down with him into prison (Wisdom 10:8). Now the passion week is at an end, for soon Joseph will be restored to life and will rise again. (AE 7:129)

So we now proceed to the end of Joseph's "passion week."

Lifted to Pharaoh's Right Hand

By comparing Genesis 37:2 and 41:46, we see that Joseph was seventeen years old when his brothers sold him into slavery and thirty years old when he was released from prison. Review all that has happened to Joseph up to this point. What does the fact that he had to wait so long for his deliverance tell you about

the way God works in the lives of His servants? Why does God often delay so long in ridding His people of their sufferings?

Review all of Genesis 41. Consider why God gave this dream to Pharaoh. Who would benefit from this dream? In what ways does this dream reveal God's concern for those outside the chosen people? What other biblical stories reveal the concern of the Lord for those outside the chosen nation? How does God still use unbelievers—including those in positions of great authority—to benefit His own people and others?

At this point in Joseph's life, he has spent about thirteen years exiled from his home country, his family, and his beloved father. Joseph was seventeen years old when he had the two dreams about being exalted over his brothers and parents (Genesis 37:2). As we are about to see, his deliverance comes when he is thirty years old (41:46). Thirteen long years he has suffered and waited! Finally, however, that for which the Lord has been preparing Joseph will become visible. His dreams are beginning to come true.

Look at the speech of the cupbearer in Genesis 41:9–13. What does he mean when he says, "I remember my offenses today"? Against whom was his offense: Pharaoh, Joseph, or others?

Genesis 41 recounts what happened. Two years after the chief cupbearer was released from prison, Pharaoh, whom he served, had two dreams. These dreams deeply troubled Pharaoh, but the "professionals"—the wise men and magicians of Egypt—could make neither hide nor hair of these dreams. Being privy to this information, the cupbearer finally broke his two-year silence.

I remember my offenses today. When Pharaoh was angry with his servants and put me and the chief baker in custody in the house of the captain of the guard, we dreamed on the same night, he and I, each having a dream with its own interpretation. A young Hebrew was there with us, a servant of the captain of the guard. When we told him, he interpreted our dreams to us, giving

an interpretation to each man according to his dream. And as he interpreted to us, so it came about. I was restored to my office, and the baker was hanged. (Genesis 41:9–13)

Though long in coming, the cupbearer finally performs his duty. He confesses his sins, describes what happened in prison, and brings to the fore the name of Joseph.

Summarize the two dreams, their interpretations, and the plan devised by Joseph. Who might Joseph have had in mind in 41:33? Describe the remarkable reversal in 41:38–43. Consider the many ways, both physical and spiritual, in which Joseph would now be able to use his office to benefit the nation.

The cupbearer's verbal résumé of Joseph presents enough credentials for the king. The inmate is fetched from jail, shaves, and dons a new suit of clothes. Joseph steps before the king, who relays his dreams and waits for an answer. It is not long in coming. The dreams, Joseph says, prophesy what will quickly come to pass in Egypt and elsewhere. Seven years of bounty will be followed by seven years of famine. Make preparations now for those bad years, Joseph counsels, by storing up a percentage of crops each good year. And, he adds, while you're at it, "Select a discerning and wise man, and set him over the land of Egypt" to make sure all this is done according to plan (Genesis 41:33). Whether Joseph had himself in mind when he offered this suggestion we cannot know. What is certain, however, is that Pharaoh recognized that Joseph was just the man for the job. Pharaoh asks,

"Can we find a man like this, in whom is the Spirit of God?" Then Pharaoh said to Joseph, "Since God has shown you all this, there is none so discerning and wise as you are. You shall be over my house, and all my people shall order themselves as you command. Only as regards the throne will I be greater than you." And Pharaoh said to Joseph, "See, I have set you over all the land of Egypt." Then Pharaoh took his signet ring from his hand and put it on Joseph's hand, and clothed him in garments of fine linen and put a gold chain about his neck. And he made him ride in his second chariot. And they called out before him, "Bow the knee!"

Thus he set him over all the land of Egypt. (Genesis 41:38–43)

What a reversal for this young man! What a testimony to the steadfast love of God, who never abandons those in need. Though God may hide Himself for a time, He is not truly absent but present—present in suffering, present in pain, present for all those downtrodden.

Joseph's ingenious plan was immediately put into action. Each of the seven years of plenty, 20 percent of the produce was put into storage. Over time, there was so much grain it could not longer be measured. It became "like the sand of the sea" (Genesis 41:49). By following Joseph's instruction, Egypt was more than prepared for the years of famine to come.

Only three conversations of Joseph are recorded during his thirteen years of captivity. In all of these, he confesses his faith and fear of God (Genesis 39:8–9; 40:8; 41:16). How might Joseph have publicly confessed his faith while serving in his new office? Read Psalm 105:16–22. In this psalm, much of the early history of Israel is described, especially the time spent in Egypt. How do these verses reflect and even expand upon the story in Genesis? In particular, what does it mean when Joseph taught the elders wisdom? What might such teaching have entailed?

But we mustn't think that Joseph was just concerned about the physical welfare of the nation. He also had in mind their spiritual welfare. He certainly showed no hesitation to confess before others the truth about God and His Word. Consider this: in the thirteen years that he was a captive, slave, or prisoner, Scripture records only three conversations that Joseph had. In all three, he confesses his faith in and fear of God (Genesis 39:8–9; 40:8; 41:16). In the last conversation, before Pharaoh himself, Joseph confessed that the interpretation of dreams is in the hands of God. Only by divine wisdom could this young Hebrew tell the king what his dreams meant and give him the necessary advice (Genesis 41:16).

Using the office into which he had been placed, Joseph could use his authority and influence to instruct the rulers and people not only about what to do with their crops, but also about the God who gave the crops in the first place. Psalm 105 says that Pharaoh made Joseph a ruler so as "to instruct his princes as he pleased and to teach his elders wisdom" (105:22 NIV). Such instruction would hardly have been limited to agricultural matters and affairs of state. Joseph preached to them the Word of God. That is the ultimate wisdom, as Joseph well knew, for he had lived by that Word for many years. Luther does not hesitate to say that under the instruction of Joseph "Pharaoh becomes a Christian," for "he is instructed in the Word of faith and true piety" (AE 7:164).

What does Luther mean when he says that Joseph is "a Christ to Egypt and even more"? How is he applying the words he quotes from John 14:12? What parallels can one draw between these two suffering servants of God? In what ways was Christ guiding and shaping the life of Joseph so that it would foreshadow His own?

As in his suffering Joseph was an "image of God's Son" (Luther), so also in his exaltation. After His crucifixion and resurrection, Jesus ascended to the right hand of the Father. From there, He reigns over the kingdom of God, His Church. He daily and richly preserves us, body and soul. After His suffering came glory, and that glory is for our good. The glory of Christ is to do good for sinners. And the good He does is our salvation. God worked in a similar way with Joseph. We have studied his prolonged "crucifixion." When that was finally over, he was exalted from the pit to sit at the right hand of Pharaoh. From there, he ruled over the kingdom of Egypt. His rule was based upon the Word and wisdom of God. It was for the good of those who suffered from famine, one of the many punishments to come upon this world because of sin. Both in worldly and spiritual matters, Joseph was doubtlessly the greatest blessing Egypt has ever known, from ancient times down to the present day. Reflecting upon how Christlike Joseph was, Luther writes,

In short, [Joseph] is a Christ to Egypt and even more, as Christ Himself says: "Truly, truly, I say

to you, he who believes in Me will also do the works that I do; and greater works than these will he do" (John 14:12). Christ converted one little nation in a corner of the one land of Judah; He fed several thousand people with a small amount of bread. Joseph fed all Egypt and the neighboring nations and kingdoms, both physically and spiritually. (AE 7:136)

Inasmuch as the Lord who was with Joseph throughout his suffering was the Son of God, we can rightly say that Christ Himself guided the life of Joseph so that it would reflect His future life.

Reconciled to His Brothers

After seven years of plenty, both Egypt and surrounding countries began to suffer the effects of the famine. Jacob and his extended family did as well. Compare 42:1–6 with 37:1–11. What has finally come to pass?

When the brothers first heard the dreams, they hated Joseph for it. They supposed it was only his self-serving self-exaltation that was in view. But what was the real purpose of Joseph being exalted to the right hand of Pharaoh? Why should the brothers have actually rejoiced when they heard of these dreams? What does such hindsight tell us about our reactions to God's ways and God's Word?

In this chapter of Joseph's life, he is finally brought face-to-face with the brothers who thrust him down the cliff of suffering. Over a dozen years had passed since they last saw "the dreamer." How had those years changed them? When they reflected back upon the crime they had committed, were they seized with remorse or filled with smugness? Such questions are answered as the rest of the story unfolds. As he embraces and forgives his brothers, we see once more how Christlike Joseph was.

The timetable foretold by Pharaoh's dreams unfolded exactly as Joseph had interpreted it. For seven years the land was fat with crops. Under Joseph's supervision, tons of grain were set aside. Thus, when the years of famine began, Egypt had food—but only Egypt. Surrounding countries were

not so fortunate. They, too, were suffering from hunger, but they had nowhere to turn, nowhere except the land of Pharaoh. Thus, from inside and outside the country, people appeared before Joseph, begging for grain.

Among those who came from outside Egypt's borders were the brothers of Joseph. Their father, Jacob, heard that there was grain for sale in Egypt, so he sent ten of his sons on a buying mission. Only Benjamin, his youngest and now favorite son, remained behind. Benjamin was the full brother of Joseph and son of Jacob's favorite wife, Rachel. When the ten brothers arrived and stood before the governor, this vice-pharaoh (as it were) of Egypt, little did they know that this "Egyptian" was in fact their little brother. Thus, little did they know that as they "came and bowed themselves before him with their faces to the ground" (42:6), the dreams that they had so hated over twenty years before had now become a reality. But Joseph knew. He recognized his brothers. No doubt his two dreams were as fresh in his mind as they were more than two decades before. God was true to His word, as Joseph knew He would be.

Scan the story in Genesis 42–45. What are the basic elements of the narrative? Why does Joseph not reveal himself to his brothers right away? What means does he employ to find out information about his family?

Joseph reveals himself to his brothers in 45:1–8. In this highly emotional scene, what kind of response does Joseph give to his brothers' treachery over twenty years earlier? What could Joseph have done to them? What prompts him to embrace his brothers the way he does? How is this action in line with Joseph's actions in Potiphar's house and in prison?

The story of how Joseph acted toward his brothers, their return trip home and second journey to Egypt, and how Joseph finally revealed himself to his brothers is recorded in Genesis 42–45. The gist of the account is that, initially, Joseph disguised himself from his brothers to assure that they would not recognize him. Then he set a plan into motion that would ensure that when his brothers returned again, they would bring Benjamin with them. And so it happened. After keeping his secret long enough, Joseph was ready to drop the Egyptian "mask" and reveal his true identity. How the emotions poured out of him at that hour! As we read,

> Then Joseph could not control himself before all those who stood by him. He cried, "Make everyone go out from me." So no one stayed with him when Joseph made himself known to his brothers. And he wept aloud, so that the Egyptians heard it, and the household of Pharaoh heard it. And Joseph said to his brothers, "I am Joseph! Is my father still alive?" (Genesis 45:1–3)

His brothers were so bewildered by the actions and words of this "Egyptian" that they were left speechless. Calling them closer, he poured out his heart before them. His words reveal that Joseph harbored no animosity toward those who had sold him into slavery. In fact, Joseph had come to realize the exact reason that God—not his brothers!—had sent him into Egypt in the first place. He resumed,

> I am your brother, Joseph, whom you sold into Egypt. And now do not be distressed or angry with yourselves because you sold me here, for God sent me before you to preserve life. For the famine has been in the land these two years, and there are yet five years in which there will be neither plowing nor harvest. And God sent me before you to preserve for you a remnant on earth, and to keep alive for you many survivors. So it was not you who sent me here, but God. He has made me a father to Pharaoh, and lord of all his house and ruler over all the land of Egypt. (Genesis 45:4–8)

What does Joseph mean when he says, "It was not you who sent me here, but God"? How are both of these statements true: The brothers sold Joseph into slavery, and God sent him down into Egypt? What does this show us about the way the Lord works in this sinful world and through sinful people?

What a confession! "It was not you who sent me here, but God." He even tells them not to be distressed or angry with themselves for the wrong they had done to him. How could Joseph say such

things? He was able to see past the treachery of his brothers, the lies of Potiphar's wife, the forgetfulness of the cupbearer; he was able to see through all these sinful, human actions to the gracious, divine hand behind all of it. The Lord of history used the deeds of sinful men and women to accomplish a great good for all of them. Indeed, the very people who hated Joseph and took advantage of him were now, as it were, reaping the good seed that Joseph had sown. The hateful brothers were eating the grain that Joseph arranged to have set aside for them. The adulterous wife of Potiphar was not starving to death because of the very man whom she once tried to lure into her bed. The cupbearer has something to put into the hand of his master because of the prisoner he finally remembered to help. All of them intended evil against Joseph or allowed such evil to continue, but God worked it out for good. He always does, without fail. For that is how God is. He transforms even the worst of evils into the greatest of goods.

Joseph's sufferings at the hands of his brothers, Potiphar's wife, and the ungrateful cupbearer were all worked into God's plan. Compare this with the life of Jesus, especially His betrayal, crucifixion, and resurrection. Use Acts 2:23 to guide you in your comparison.

Read Joseph's words in 45:7. Joseph's mission was a mission of life, but it was hidden beneath many "deaths" that he had to suffer. Even though the ultimate goal of Joseph's sufferings had been prophesied in his dreams, it wasn't clear how God would work everything out until Joseph was exalted to the right hand of Pharaoh. How in this is Joseph also an "image of God's Son" (Luther)? How did the resurrection of Jesus finally shed light on all the prior sufferings He had endured?

Once again we see the kinship between Joseph and Jesus. What greater human evil has ever been perpetrated than the hatred, rejection, and crucifixion of the Son of God? What is more horrific than sinners spitting in the face of the Almighty, killing Him, and mocking Him as He slowly dies? Yet, how was God active in all this? The same way He was in the evils committed against Joseph. Our heavenly Father used these deeds of sinful men and women to accomplish the greatest of goods for all of them—their salvation. In his Pentecost sermon, the apostle Peter describes it this way: "This Jesus, delivered up according to the definite plan and foreknowledge of God, you crucified and killed by the hands of lawless men" (Acts 2:23). Thus it was no accident that Jesus was crucified. It happened according to the "definite plan and foreknowledge of God." At the same time, the Jews crucified and killed Him "by the hands of lawless men." God was at work in and through sinners to bring about good for these sinners.

Joseph testifies to his brothers that God sent him before them down into Egypt "to preserve life . . . [and] to preserve for you a remnant on earth, and to keep alive for you many survivors" (Genesis 45:5, 7). The mission of Joseph was thus a mission of life. By means of his plan, the physical lives of thousands of people were saved. And, by means of his teaching and instruction in the Word of God, there is no telling how many sinners were brought to faith and everlasting life in the Messiah. What great wonders our Father in heaven worked through this man!

There is also another way in which we see Joseph as an "image of God's Son": in his compassion toward those who had done so many evils against him. When his brothers arrived in Egypt, Joseph had the power to put them to death. No one would have batted an eye had he done so. If it were revenge he sought, then he had the perfect opportunity. But Joseph did not exact revenge against them. In fact, he even tells the wrongdoers not to be distressed or angry with themselves over selling him into slavery (Genesis 45:5). He forgives them, even as he no doubt had forgiven Potiphar's wife and the cupbearer.

How did Joseph react to his brothers' words (Genesis 50:17–21)? How is Joseph a Christ-figure to his brothers?

Years later, after Joseph had brought all his family down to Egypt and settled them there, his father, Jacob, died at the age of 147 years (Genesis 47:28).

It had been seventeen years since Joseph first revealed himself to, forgave, and began to lavish blessings upon these very brothers who had lavished nothing but evil upon him during the first seventeen years of his life. Still, they were nervous. Seventeen years of compassion and love from Joseph were still not enough to calm their trembling consciences.

> When Joseph's brothers saw that their father was dead, they said, "It may be that Joseph will hate us and pay us back for all the evil that we did to him." So they sent a message to Joseph, saying, "Your father gave this command before he died, 'Say to Joseph, Please forgive the transgression of your brothers and their sin, because they did evil to you.' And now, please forgive the transgression of the servants of the God of your father." (Genesis 50:15–17)

Joseph arranged to have his father and all his family brought down to Egypt. Jacob lived another seventeen years with Joseph (47:28). During this time, Joseph did everything he could to take care of his father, his brothers, and their families. Yet when their father died, the brothers of Joseph were afraid of Joseph. Read Genesis 50:15–17. What did they think Joseph would now do? What were they accusing Joseph of doing the past seventeen years? What does this reveal about their own consciences? Do you agree that there is nothing harder to believe than that your sins are forgiven free of charge? Why or why not?

One doubts whether Jacob really gave this command to his sons. We cannot be sure. Whether he did or did not, however, it reveals that the brothers were still deeply troubled over their sin. They could not see how someone to whom they had done such wrong could return nothing but good to them. "It must all be for show," they thought. "Joseph can't really be that forgiving, that patient, that full of love for us. After all, what we have deserved is the exact opposite."

That is the way the sinful heart works. The truth is, there is nothing harder to believe than "Your sins are forgiven." Nothing seems more preposterous than to trust that Christ absolves us with no strings attached, with no requirements, no demands, nothing but pure grace. So frequently we confess the same sins over and over, each time needing to hear once more, "I love you. I forgive you. You are mine." Yet Christ is ready and willing to do that. For He died and rose again not only to earn our forgiveness but to put that forgiveness into us as many times as necessary, in as many ways as necessary.

So it was with Joseph. For seventeen years, Joseph demonstrated time and again that he did not hate his brothers but loved and forgave them. Still, he was willing to repeat this once again.

> *Joseph wept when they spoke to him. His brothers also came and fell down before him and said, "Behold, we are your servants." But Joseph said to them, "Do not fear, for am I in the place of God? As for you, you meant evil against me, but God meant it for good, to bring it about that many people should be kept alive, as they are today. So do not fear; I will provide for you and your little ones." Thus he comforted them and spoke kindly to them. (Genesis 50:17–21)*

Since the brothers are so frightened that Joseph will finally seek vengeance, not once but twice he says to them, "Do not fear." As he told them seventeen years ago, he confirms again that all this happened not willy-nilly but according to God's divine plan. Yes, he says, you meant evil against me, but that is not what is most important. What really mattered was that God meant it for good. His goal was accomplished that many people should be kept alive due to the wisdom and foresight of Joseph. Repeating his admonition not to be afraid, Joseph adds that he will take care of his brothers and their families. Thus, Joseph does not want a pound of their flesh; in fact, his desire is to supply whatever they need, to put his brotherly love into action, which he had been doing all along anyway.

In doing so, Joseph modeled the kind of compassion and love extended toward us sinners by our Lord Jesus Christ. Of course, the kindness of Jesus is much greater than that of Joseph—Jesus is Love itself! But we nonetheless see in the actions of Joseph a prefiguring of how the "Greater Joseph" will deal with us. No matter how many times we have acted toward our Lord the way the brothers acted toward Joseph, He never stops forgiving, loving, and welcoming us back. No matter how heinous the crime, how perverse the deed, how hateful the word, it makes no difference with Jesus. He died for all. He died specifically for you. Unlike Joseph, He will not protest, "Am I in the place of God?" For in fact, He is in the place of God. He is God. Yet He is the God who would rather endure suffering and death than spend an eternity without you. That is the kind of God you have. That is how much He wants to have you as His own. Thus, in the very place of God, He says, "I forgive you. You intended evil against Me, but I intend nothing but good for you. Fear not. I love you. Again, I say, fear not, I will provide for you forgiveness, life, and salvation. I will care for you in this life and in the life to come."

Conclusion

We said at the beginning of lesson 1 that Joseph's life was a sort of dream come true, but all too often it seemed more like a nightmare. As a suffering servant of God and of his fellow men, Joseph endured many and various crosses. Family hatred, rejection because of God's Word, separation from his father, slavery, false accusations, unjust imprisonment, forgetful "friends": you name it and Joseph suffered it. But in the end, it became clear why. The Lord was shaping him for the important task that lay ahead. God had sent him to be a savior for Egypt and many other nearby countries. So after his many "crucifixions," he was raised from the dungeon to save lives. And in his exalted position, he acted out of love and compassion, even toward those who had wronged him most.

In all these things—both what he suffered and what he did out of love—Joseph was what Luther called an "image of God's Son." Our heavenly Father so ordered Joseph's life that it would be a sketch of the life that Jesus would live. These events were written down for our sakes, that we might read this life story of Joseph as a sort of "Old Testament Gospel," with Joseph as the Christ-character. Thanks be to God that we see manifested in the life of Joseph the kind of love and forgiveness granted to us in Jesus. In Christ we do not have merely an image—we have the real thing.

Closing Prayer

Almighty God, You know we live in the midst of so many dangers that in our frailty we cannot stand upright. Grant strength and protection to support us in all dangers and carry us through all temptations; through Jesus Christ, Your Son, our Lord, who lives and reigns with You and the Holy Spirit, one God, now and forever. Amen.

(Collect for Epiphany 4, *Lutheran Service Book*)

INSIDE EGYPT
JOSEPH

Falsely Accused:

Read **Genesis 39:1–20**.

Describe Joseph's situation in Egypt. What happened to him once he arrived? Contrast his life in Egypt under Potiphar with what his life had been like while still at home. What kinds of temptations might he have faced in Egypt: doubt, despair, loneliness?

What kind of servant was Joseph? What did his master think of him? What does this reveal about Joseph and the attitude he adopted regarding his new situation? What does this reveal about his hope and his faith?

How did Satan use the wife of Potiphar to tempt Joseph? What does this show us about the way the devil works? What would have been Satan's ultimate goal?

How did Joseph respond to her repeated advances? Analyze his response. What reasons does Joseph give for refusing her? What else could Joseph have said? What eventually happens with Potiphar's wife? How was Joseph "rewarded" for his faithful service?

Compare this incident in the life of Joseph with the various false accusations leveled against Jesus. In what ways were both men faithful to the task given them by God? What kinds of accusations were leveled against Jesus? See **Matthew**

9:34; **11:19**; **26:65**; and **27:29**. How did both of these men react?

Where was God when both Joseph and Jesus were suffering? Why does God allow such sufferings to befall His servants? How does God use pain, grief, and loss in our lives in a similar way?

Interpreting in Prison . . . and Being Forgotten

What seems to have happened to Joseph's life? As he reflected upon the dreams he had while still with his father, what kinds of thoughts would the devil have planted in his mind? Read **Hebrews 11:1**. Apply these words to Joseph's situation. What did it mean for him, in his particular situation, to live by faith?

Compare Joseph's service in Potiphar's house with his service in prison. How are they similar? How did Joseph fare in prison?

Summarize what the baker and cupbearer dreamed. Read **Genesis 40:8**. What is Joseph claiming? If all interpretations belong to God, how could Joseph promise to interpret the dreams? What does this tell us about the way Joseph viewed his relationship with God? How was Joseph the spokesman for the Lord?

Read **Genesis 40:14–15**. What is Joseph's request? Is he justified in making this request? Why or why not?

The cupbearer is seemingly the only one who could act to have Joseph released, yet what does he do (**40:23**)? Reading ahead, note for how long the cupbearer kept silent about what Joseph had done for him (**41:1**)? Put yourself in Joseph's shoes: What would this period of waiting have been like for him?

In what ways is the forgetfulness of the cupbearer typical of sinful humans? How do we treat those who have done good things for us? How do we oftentimes shirk our responsibilities to help others, even if they have formerly assisted us?

Once more, what kind of temptations would have faced Joseph in this situation?

Luther writes: "The very saintly and good Joseph was crucified, died, was buried, and descended into hell during these two years" (AE 7:129). Luther is obviously not speaking literally but is comparing the sufferings of Joseph and Jesus. In what ways are they similar? How can we speak of this time as a "crucifixion" for Joseph? Read **Matthew 27:46**. What does this cry of Jesus mean? How might Joseph have prayed similarly?

Lifted to Pharaoh's Right Hand

By comparing **Genesis 37:2** and **41:46**, we see that Joseph was seventeen years old when his brothers sold him into slavery and thirty years old when he was released from prison. Review all that has happened to Joseph up to this point. What does the fact that he had to wait so long for his deliverance tell you about the way God works in the lives of His servants? Why does God often delay so long in ridding His people of their sufferings?

Review all of **Genesis 41**. Consider why God gave this dream to Pharaoh. Who would benefit from this dream? In what ways does this dream reveal God's concern for those outside the chosen people? What other biblical stories reveal the concern of the Lord for those outside the chosen nation? How does God still use unbelievers—including those in positions of great authority—to benefit His own people and others?

Look at the speech of the cupbearer in **Genesis 41:9–13**. What does he mean when he says, "I remember my offenses today"? Against whom was his offense: Pharaoh, Joseph, or others?

Summarize the two dreams, their interpretations, and the plan devised by Joseph. Who might Joseph have had in mind in **41:33**? Describe the remarkable reversal in **41:38–43**. Consider the many ways, both physical and spiritual, in which Joseph would now be able to use his office to benefit the nation.

Only three conversations of Joseph are recorded during his thirteen years of captivity. In all of these, he confesses his faith and fear of God (**Genesis 39:8–9**; **40:8**; **41:16**). How might Joseph have publicly confessed his faith while serving in his new office? Read **Psalm 105:16–22**. In this psalm, much of the early history of Israel is described, especially the time spent in Egypt. How do these verses reflect and even expand upon the story in Genesis? In particular, what does it mean when Joseph taught the elders wisdom? What might such teaching have entailed?

Consider these words of Luther concerning Joseph:

*In short, [Joseph] is a Christ in Egypt and even more, as Christ Himself says: "Truly, truly, I say to you, he who believes in Me will also do the works that I do; and greater works than these will he do" (**John 14:12**). Christ converted one little nation in a corner of the one land of Judah; He fed several thousand people with a small amount of bread. Joseph fed all Egypt and the* *neighboring nations and kingdoms, both physically and spiritually. (AE 7:136)*

What does Luther mean when he says that Joseph is "a Christ in Egypt and even more"? How is he applying the words he quotes from **John 14:12**? What parallels can one draw between these two suffering servants of God? In what ways was Christ guiding and shaping the life of Joseph so that it would foreshadow His own?

Reconciled to His Brothers

After seven years of plenty, both Egypt and surrounding countries began to suffer the effects of the famine. Jacob and his extended family did as well. Compare **42:1–6** with **37:1–11**. What has finally come to pass?

When the brothers first heard the dreams, they hated Joseph for it. They supposed it was only his self-serving self-exaltation that was in view. But what was the real purpose of Joseph's being exalted to the right hand of Pharaoh? Why should the brothers have actually rejoiced when they heard of these dreams? What does such hindsight tell us about our reactions to God's ways and God's Word?

Scan the story in **Genesis 42–45**. What are the basic elements of the narrative? Why does Joseph not reveal himself to his brothers right away? What means does he employ to find out information about his family?

Joseph reveals himself to his brothers in **45:1–8**. In this highly emotional scene, what kind of response does Joseph give to his brother's treachery over twenty years earlier? What could Joseph have done to them? What prompts him to embrace his brothers the way he does? How is this action in line with Joseph's actions in Potiphar's house and in prison?

What does Joseph mean when he says, "It was not you who sent me here, but God"? How are both of these state-ments true: The brothers sold Joseph into slavery, and God sent him down into Egypt? What does this show us about the way the Lord works in this sinful world and through sinful people?

Joseph's sufferings at the hands of his brothers, Potiphar's wife, and the ungrateful cupbearer were all worked into God's plan. Compare this with the life of Jesus, especially His betrayal, crucifixion, and resurrection. Use **Acts 2:23** to guide you in your comparison.

Read Joseph's words in **45:7**. Joseph's mission was a mission of life, but it was hidden beneath many "deaths" that he had to suffer. Even though the ultimate goal of Joseph's sufferings had been prophesied in his dreams, it wasn't clear how God would work everything out until Joseph was exalted to the right hand of Pharaoh. How in this is Joseph also an "image of God's Son" (Luther)? How did the resurrection of Jesus finally shed light on all the prior sufferings He had endured?

How did Joseph react to his brothers' words (**Genesis 50:17–21**)? How is Joseph a Christ-figure to his brothers?

Joseph arranged to have his father and all his family brought down to Egypt. Jacob lived another seventeen years with Joseph (**47:28**). During this time, Joseph did everything he could to take care of his father, his brothers, and their families. Yet when their father died, the brothers of Joseph were afraid of Joseph. Read **Genesis 50:15–17**. What did they think Joseph would now do? What were they accusing Joseph of doing the past seventeen years? What does this reveal about their own consciences? Do you agree that there is nothing harder to believe than that your sins are forgiven free of charge? Why or why not?

OUT OF EGYPT MOSES

Opening Prayer

Almighty and everlasting God, mercifully look upon our infirmities and stretch forth the hand of Your majesty to heal and defend us; through Jesus Christ, Your Son, our Lord, who lives and reigns with You and the Holy Spirit, one God, now and forever. Amen.

(Collect for Epiphany 3, *Lutheran Service Book*).

Moses—Suffering Savior

What images spring to mind when the name *Moses* is mentioned? Are they positive or negative? What overall portrait of him stands out in your mind?

The image that almost always springs to mind when the name *Moses* is mentioned is that of a long-bearded, robe-wearing, sour-faced fellow who's holding high two big chunks of rock with the Ten Commandments chiseled into them. He looks like he's ready to smash them on the ground . . . or into someone's head! That's the Moses most people

know and, well, *don't* love. He's stern. He's inflexible. He looks mighty ticked off about something. That's Moses.

However, that's *not* Moses. Or, at least, it is a very twisted image of him, based on a single incident when, in fact, he was mighty mad about something—and rightly so! The real Moses won't fit in the box we try to squeeze him into. He's a complex character. He can be very stern, to be sure, but also very gentle and compassionate. No more humble man walked the earth in his day (Numbers 12:3). He is concerned about others, especially the downtrodden. For the sake of others, he sacrifices himself. He is more, much more, than the negative caricature often associated with him.

The life of Moses is easily divided into three forty-year segments. Until the age of forty, he lived in Egypt. From age forty to eighty, he lived in Midian with his father-in-law and family. And from age eighty to one hundred twenty he pastored the Israelite congregation. Think of the various offices and vocations Moses had during these 120 years. From

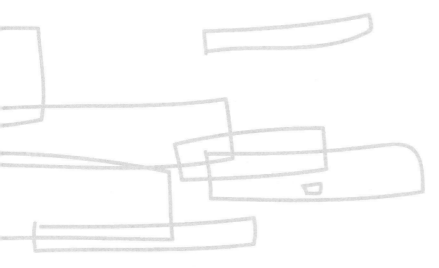

what you recall of his life story, what are some major ways in which the Lord called him to bear a cross?

On Moses' final birthday, 120 candles covered the cake. We know a little about his first forty years, very little about the next forty, and plenty about what happened from his eightieth birthday on. One thing that we know for certain is that many of these years were far from a walk in the park. Moses didn't make it past his first birthday before his life was in danger. Around the time he turned forty, he had to flee Egypt lest Pharaoh have him executed. And when he turned eighty, instead of retiring to a life of ease, he was sent to pastor the Israelite congregation out of Egypt and into the Promised Land. To make matters worse, this congregation wanted to kill him about as often as they wanted to follow him!

Like Joseph, Moses is one of the suffering servants in the Scriptures. If Joseph suffered much in the process of getting the Israelites into Egypt, then Moses suffered just as much getting them out of Egypt and back to Joseph's homeland. Though most people see Moses as more of a lawgiver, he was

first and foremost a deliverer. God sent him to deliver Israel, to lead His people out of captivity. Moses did so, but he bore dozens of crosses along the way.

The four evangelists often draw connections between Moses and Jesus. We'll be looking at some of these in the pages that follow. In this lesson, we'll see that what was true of Joseph is also true of Moses—that many incidents of suffering in his life are a foreshadowing of our Lord's sufferings. As the Lord of history, Christ so arranged the life of Moses that it would reflect His own. Jesus therefore comes to repeat and complete what Moses endured. In so doing, He shows us that sacred history comes to fulfillment in Him. What was shown only in part in the sufferings of Joseph, Moses, and many others is shown in full in the sufferings of our Lord.

Infant Murder

Read Exodus 1. How did the Israelites prosper in Egypt for a time? What led to problems with Pharaoh? What was this Egyptian ruler worried about? He tried three different ways to

slow down or decimate the Israelite population. What are these three, and did they succeed? Tertullian, a Church father, once remarked that the blood of the martyrs is the seed of the Church. In what way would this apply to the Israelite situation as well?

When baby Moses exited his mother's womb, a guillotine blade was hanging over his neck, ready to fall. It was the worst of times, especially for infant boys. What led up to this? For several generations, Moses' people, the Israelites, had experienced a "baby boom" in Egypt. The Hebrew literally says the land "swarmed" with them (Exodus 1:7). This population explosion not only caught Pharaoh's attention, it worried him greatly. He fretted that if an enemy army invaded his land, the Israelite settlers might become turncoats and aid in Egypt's defeat.

Pharaoh's political anxiety called for decisive action, so he tried three different ways to slow down the population increase. First, he attempted to work the Israelites to death, or at least to have fewer babies, but that plan didn't work so well. In fact, it backfired badly, so that "the more [the Israelites] were oppressed, the more they multiplied and the more they spread abroad" (Exodus 1:12). Strike one. Next, the king commanded the midwives of the Hebrew women to snuff out the life of any male infant as soon as he left his mother. This plan also miscarried, for the midwives feared God more than the huffing and puffing of Pharaoh. Strike two. The third time, however, was a home run, or so it seemed to the Egyptians. The king enacted state-sponsored infanticide—baby murder. By law, every son born to the Hebrews was to be fed alive to the Nile River.

Pharaoh and the Egyptians did these horrible things to the people of God. What did many of the Israelites likely think about God's concern (or lack of concern) over their predicament? This persecution of the people of God was one of many persecutions of the Church that happened in the Scriptures (and, of course, that continue to happen today). Why does God allow His Church to endure such afflictions? Do we even know why? What would God have the Church do during such times?

The Israelites likely wondered why God was allowing this ongoing persecution of His chosen people. Sadly we see this persecution of the people of God throughout the Scriptures and the annals of world history. While we may never completely understand why God allows such affliction, we do know that the root cause is sin in the world. During these times of persecution, God would have us patiently endure, trusting in His divine rescue in His own time.

Read Exodus 2:1–10. The mother of Moses tried to hide him for three months, we are told, because she saw that he was a "fine" child (2:2). Some translations say that she saw he was a "beautiful" child. Why does this seem like a strange reason for a mother to hide her child? The Hebrew word variously translated "beautiful" or "fine" is literally "good." This is the same word that occurs seven times in Genesis 1 as "good" or "very good." Think of Moses in relation to the "good" in Genesis 1. How might this tell us something about God's future plans for this child? How does Moses fit into God's "good" plan for creation?

When the mother of Moses places him into the Nile, how do we see God's invisible hand at work? How does He providentially direct everything to work out for Moses?

During these frightful years, Moses was born. His mother, we are told, hid her baby for three months rather than follow the murderous order of Pharaoh (Exodus 2:2). The stated reason she did so, however, is not what we might expect. The Scripture doesn't say "because she loved him" or "because she feared God"—though both were surely true—but because "she saw that he was a fine child" (2:2). The Hebrew word translated as "fine" is literally "good." It is hard not to hear an echo of Genesis 1 in this description of the boy. Seven times in that chapter the Lord sees what He had made and pronounces it "good" or "very good." Moses, too, is "good." He is the Lord's handiwork, crafted by Him for something very special. He was a Godsend to Israel, born to be the one who would lead them to freedom.

At the end of three months, the mother couldn't hide the boy any longer. The story of her actions is recorded in Exodus 2:3–10. To summarize, she crafted a tiny ark for him, set the floating cradle in the Nile, and sent along the baby's sister to see what would happen. The Lord so arranged it that—of all people—Pharaoh's daughter found the basket, had pity on the boy, and adopted him as her own son. Thanks to the quick interjection by Miriam, Moses' own mother served as his wet nurse until he was weaned, after which time he moved under the roof of the very king who had been more of a Hitler to him than an adopted grandfather.

In a moment, we'll compare these goings-on to similar events in the early years of Jesus. Before we do so, however, in order to set the stage for a complete comparison, we need to fast-forward a bit in Moses' life.

Between his infancy and his fortieth year, where was Moses? In Acts 7:22, what does Stephen tell us Moses was doing during this first stage of his life? In what way would the skills acquired during these years have been of assistance to him in later years?

In Exodus 2:11, we are told that Moses went out to see "his people"? What does this tell us about Moses' knowledge of his background?

After Moses killed the Egyptian, he fled to Midian, where he remained for the next forty years, until he was eighty years old. Exodus 2:15–4:20 describe Moses' flight to Midian, his marriage, his call from God to deliver Israel, and his return. Briefly review the events in this chapter.

Until the age of forty, Moses resided in the palace. He was "instructed in all the wisdom of the Egyptians, and he was mighty in his words and deeds" (Acts 7:22). He did know, however, who he really was—an Israelite. One day, while paying a visit to his oppressed people, he saw an Egyptian beating an Israelite. Seeing no one else around, Moses defended the slave by striking down the Egyptian and hiding his corpse in the sand. The next day,

while breaking up a quarrel between two Israelites, one of them smarted off, "Who made you a prince and a judge over us? Do you mean to kill me as you killed the Egyptian?" (Exodus 2:14). Moses not only realized his deed was now public knowledge; even the king had heard about it and "sought to kill Moses" (2:15). So, straightway he ran away from Egypt. On the lam for the next forty years, Moses would return to his homeland only when he was eighty (Acts 7:30), when all the men who sought his life were dead (Exodus 4:19).

There are several similarities between Moses and Jesus regarding what was done to them while they were infants. In fact, in Matthew's Gospel, he assumes that his readers know the story of Exodus 1–4, for he uses language from this account to describe what happened to Jesus. Read Matthew 2, note the parallels between these two infancy narratives, and comment on their significance.

Needless to say, by the time he reached his eightieth birthday, Moses had some tales of danger and suffering to tell. In fact, he did tell them, writing with his own hand the story of his nativity, upbringing, and flight from Egypt in Exodus 2. Every Israelite knew these stories like the back of their hand, as indeed, Christians should as well. In fact, one of the evangelists, St. Matthew, assumes his readers are well-acquainted with this story, for it is against the background of Moses' life that he writes of events in the early life of Jesus. As we shall see, both Moses and Jesus, long before they were out of diapers, were already true suffering servants of the heavenly Father.

Compare the two rulers: Herod and Pharaoh. What did they do, and what drove them to do what they did? Israel was in captivity in Egypt when Moses was born. Under what kind of political and spiritual captivity was Israel when Jesus was born? Note Luke 2:1 and John 8:34.

Like Moses' people, at the time Jesus was born, His people were under the thumb of a powerful overlord. For Moses it was the Egyptians, but for

Jesus it was the Romans. They ruled the Jews. In fact, it was because of a Roman census that the mother and stepfather of Jesus ended up in Bethlehem at the time of His delivery (Luke 2:1–5). Over the region in which Jesus was born, power was wielded by a particularly bloodthirsty, heartless despot named Herod. He, like Pharaoh, would decree the murder of infant boys.

It happened like this. Around two years or less after Jesus' nativity, the Magi arrived in Jerusalem from the East, having trailed the star that pointed to the birth of the king of the Jews (Matthew 2). When Herod heard of their mission, he called them in, put on a pious face, and learned from them the details of their journey. When the Wise Men completed their journey to Bethlehem and headed homeward without informing Herod of the exact whereabouts of the child, he was furious. Not only had he been tricked, but Herod sensed political danger in this infant "king of the Jews"—a rival to his office! Like Pharaoh of old, Herod went for the jugular. He "sent and killed all the male children in Bethlehem and in all that region who were two years old or under, according to the time that he has ascertained from the wise men" (Matthew 2:16). The Nile River "flooded" into the nurseries of Bethlehem.

Compare Herod's slaughter of the children in Bethlehem with Pharaoh's attempt to eradicate the male children of the Israelites. What means did God employ to save both Moses and Jesus?

But where was Jesus during this horrific slaughter? Like the chosen child Moses, Jesus had been rescued from this mass infant execution by the grace and providence of the heavenly Father. Before the soldiers arrived, "an angel of the Lord appeared to Joseph in a dream and said, 'Rise, take the child and His mother, and flee to Egypt, and remain there until I tell you, for Herod is about to search for the child, to destroy Him.' And he rose and took the child and His mother by night and departed to Egypt and remained there until the death of Herod" (Matthew 2:13–15).

Thus while boys around them were murdered

by cruel tyrants, both Moses and Jesus were saved—delivered in order to be deliverers themselves! Their future lay entirely in the hand of God. And in that hand they were safe. Quite amazingly, the haven of refuge for Moses was right under the nose of Pharaoh. Also amazingly, for Jesus safety was found nowhere else but in the very land where Moses was born and reared!

Jesus remained in Egypt with Mary and Joseph until when? Read Matthew 2:19–20. Compare these verses with Exodus 4:19. Note the similarities in the verses. By imitating Exodus, Matthew wants you, a hearer of his Gospel, to think in a certain way about Jesus. What is this way? Why would he want you to think of Jesus as a sort of new Moses?

There remains one more parallel to point out between these two incidents. As noted above, around his fortieth birthday, Moses was forced to flee from Pharaoh, this time for killing an Egyptian. He did not return to set his people free from captivity until those who sought his life were dead (Exodus 4:19). It was similar with Jesus. He remained in Egypt, away from the murderous grasp of Herod, for some time. He did not return to the land where His people were captive until the coast was clear. When Matthew describes that return, he reveals in his choice of language that he is consciously imitating the story of Moses' own return. Compare these two verses.

Exodus 4:19:

"The LORD said to Moses in Midian, 'Go back to Egypt, for all the men who were seeking your life are dead.' So Moses took his wife and his sons and had them ride on a donkey, and went back to the land of Egypt."

Matthew 2:20:

[An angel told Joseph,] "'Rise, take the child and His mother and go to the land of Israel, for those who sought the child's life are dead.' And he rose and took the child and his mother and went to the land of Israel."

How can one not hear an echo resounding from Exodus to Matthew? Christian artists have certainly heard it. If you are familiar with depictions of the

"Flight of the Holy Family into Egypt," you may recall that Joseph is usually pictured leading a donkey, atop of which sits Mary with Jesus in her arms. The artists caught the connection! The two stories are, as it were, merged into one in the portrait. Moses returned to his people, to lead them out of slavery to the new life God had promised them. Jesus, too, was returning to His people, to lead them out of the slavery of sin and death to the new life God had promised them, which Jesus Himself would earn and bestow. Both of these deliverers began infancy as suffering servants. But the Lord was on their side. He saved them from the tyrants' murderous decrees, for they were essential to His plan for the life of the people He loved.

Rejected by the People He Came to Save

When we studied the life of Joseph, we saw how he was rejected and hated by the very ones whom God called him to deliver from death. Moses also—and virtually every suffering servant in the Bible—was stiff-armed by the same people he was sent to save. In this respect, we see Moses as an "image of God's Son." For though "God so loved the world that He gave His only begotten Son" (John 3:16 KJV), the world so hated God that they rejected His Son, hated Him, and mocked and murdered Him. As Jesus says to His brothers, "The world cannot hate you, but it hates Me because I testilfy about it, that its works are evil." (John 7:7). Again speaking to His disciples the Lord says, "If the world hates you, know that it has hated Me before it hated you" (John 15:18). But the Lord is merciful and gracious. Though we rejected Him, He reconciled us. Though we killed, He forgave. The very blood we shed, He caused to become the blood of atonement for us. The world's sinful rejection of the Son was used by God as the means of accepting us sinners as His own children.

Moses suffered rejection at the hands of his countrymen in many different ways, on many different occasions. We will highlight only a couple of them.

Who Do You Think You Are? —Rejected Right Away

Like Joseph and Jesus, Moses suffered rejection from his countrymen in many ways. Reflect upon how God does not let these rejections spoil His plans for the salvation of His people. What does this tell us about the character of the Lord and His will for sinful humanity?

Read again Exodus 2:11–14. Why does Moses kill the Egyptian? Does this appear to be legitimate? Why or why not?

Some have been critical of this action, claiming Moses was acting rashly. Read Acts 7:23–28. What does verse 25 tell us about Moses' motivation and assumption when he killed the Egyptian? If Moses already knew that God had chosen him to deliver the Israelites, how does this affect our interpretation of his killing of the Egyptian?

Read Exodus 2:14 and Acts 7:26–29. Compare these two accounts of the same incident. What does Stephen add in Acts 7 that is not explicit in Exodus 2. The next day, what reaction do the Israelites have to Moses? How are the Israelites not only rejecting Moses, but God as well?

When we covered some of the incidents in the early life of Moses, we briefly summarized what happened on the day Moses killed the Egyptian who was beating the Hebrew slave, as well as what transpired the next day. Moses records the account:

One day, when Moses had grown up, he went out to his people and looked on their burdens, and he saw an Egyptian beating a Hebrew, one of his people. He looked this way and that, and seeing no one, he struck down the Egyptian and hid him in the sand. When he went out the next day, behold, two Hebrews were struggling together. And he said to the man in the wrong, "Why do you strike your companion?" He answered, "Who made you a prince and a judge over us? Do you mean to kill me as you killed the Egyptian?" Then Moses was afraid and thought, "Surely the thing is known." When Pharaoh heard of it, he sought to kill Moses. But Moses fled from Pharaoh and stayed in the land of Midian. (Exodus 2:11–15)

On the surface, it looks as if this action by Moses was not only rash but unlawful. Even if the man was beating the slave, Moses took the law into his own hands in killing the Egyptian. Thus Moses shouldn't have been surprised that the next day some Hebrew smart aleck asked if he was going to kill him too.

But we need to look below the surface to discern what Moses was actually doing and what prompted him to act in this way. This below the surface meaning is brought out by Stephen in his speech to the Jews in Acts 7, part of which reads:

When [Moses] was forty years old, it came into his heart to visit his brothers, the children of Israel. And seeing one of them being wronged, he defended the oppressed man and avenged him by striking down the Egyptian. He supposed that his brothers would understand that God was giving them salvation by his hand, but they did not understand. (vv. 23–25)

Note well that last sentence. Moses didn't just fly off the handle. He did not kill the enemy either from malice or sheer passion. Rather, as Stephen affirms, Moses supposed that the Israelites would discern in his actions that he was their savior, sent by God to free them from the likes of this Egyptian. But they didn't get it. As an example of their failure to understand, Stephen relates the rejection Moses faced on the morrow:

And on the following day [Moses] appeared to them as they were quarreling and tried to reconcile them, saying, "Men, you are brothers. Why do you wrong each other?" But the man who was wronging his neighbor thrust him aside, saying, "Who made you a ruler and a judge over us? Do you want to kill me as you killed the Egyptian yesterday?" At this retort Moses fled and became an exile in the line of Midian. (Acts 7:26–29)

Stephen gives us eyes to see what was in the mind of Moses. He was thinking something like this:

God has selected me to free His people from slavery, to give them salvation. I refuse to be called a son of Pharaoh's daughter. I choose

instead to be mistreated with the people of God than to enjoy the fleeting pleasures of sin with the Egyptians (Hebrews 11:24–25). Thus, today, I will slay this enemy and, in so doing, I will demonstrate to them that I am the one whom God has ordained to be their deliverer.

In spite of Moses' best intentions, however, the whole thing blew up in his face. As they say, "No good deed goes unpunished." When Moses tried to make peace the next day, the Hebrew bully thrust him aside and sneered, "Who made you a ruler and a judge over us?" In other words, "Hey, Moses, who do you think you are? Gonna murder me too?"

There is a twofold rejection in the words of this scoffer: a rejection of God and of His servant. This man neither believes that the Lord sent Moses nor that Moses is fulfilling God's will. He slanders Moses as a self-appointed, pseudo-deliverer whose only real goal is bloodshed. Thus Moses is given the cold shoulder by the same people he came to save.

In what way is this initial rejection of Moses a preview of how they act toward him in the future? The Israelite essentially accuses Moses of planning murder against him. Read Exodus 14:10–12; 16:1–3; 17:1–3; Numbers 20:2–13; 21:1–9. In what future contexts do you hear an echo of this initial accusation that Moses was a killer?

Look at other times when the leadership of Moses was questioned. Who opposed Moses, for instance, in Numbers 12:1–16? What happened in Numbers 14:1–4? Who opposed the leadership of Moses in Numbers 16? How do similar problems still emerge in the Church today?

Echoes of this initial rejection of Moses reverberate throughout the rest of his life, especially the accusation that he was really out to slay Israelites. At the Red Sea, the people charged him with bringing them out of Egypt only to kill them (Exodus 14:10–12). When their stomachs were empty or their throats dry, they claimed he was trying to kill everyone with hunger (16:1–3) or thirst (17:1–3; Numbers 20:2–13; 21:1–9).

Time and again, they also questioned whether

Moses was really the ruler and judge whom God appointed over Israel. His own brother and sister, Aaron and Miriam, once opposed his leadership (Numbers 12:1–16). When they reached the Promised Land the first time and chickened out when they saw that the inhabitants looked like NFL linebackers, they wanted to choose another leader and go back to Egypt (Numbers 14:1–4). Later, some of them claimed equal authority with Moses, and were punished by God (Numbers 16). Therefore, the initial slap in the face by his people was certainly not the last assault against him. This "who do you think you are" attitude would be perpetuated until this divinely called leader breathed his last on the outskirts of the Promised Land.

The rejection of Moses and his call from God to be Israel's leader and deliverer was the same sort of rejection endured by Jesus as well. This should have come as no surprise to those who knew about the prophecies of the Messiah. What do these passages tell us about how the Messiah will or will not be received: Psalm 118:22 (see Matthew 21:42) and Isaiah 52:13–53:12?

As it was with Moses, so it was also with our Lord Jesus. He met rejection every step of His journey, from Bethlehem to Calvary. The fact that the Messiah would receive such treatment was no surprise, however, at least for those who knew the Scriptures. Every time Psalm 118 was chanted, for instance, the worshipers said of the Messiah, "The stone that the builders rejected has become the cornerstone" (Psalm 118:22; Matthew 21:42). Isaiah also preached, "He was despised and rejected by men; a man of sorrows, and acquainted with grief; and as one from whom men hide their faces He was despised, and we esteemed Him not" (53:3). The Anointed One would hardly be accepted with open arms.

Moses was rejected on the first occasion in which he showed himself to be Israel's deliverer. What happened to Jesus when He publicly preached that He was the Deliverer sent from the Father (Luke 4:16–30)? How was the divine authority of Jesus questioned? See John 2:18 and Matthew 21:23. Of what did they accuse Jesus in Matthew 12:22–32?

Just as Moses was disbelieved on the first occasion in which he made his divine office known, so also with Jesus. When Jesus preached at his "home congregation" in Nazareth near the beginning of His ministry, Jesus publicly declared that He was the Messiah, sent from the Father to redeem Israel. The response? His hearers were "filled with wrath" and tried to throw Him down a cliff (Luke 4:16–30)! Likewise, His messianic office was questioned over and over. If to Moses they said, "Who made you a prince and a judge over us?" (Exodus 2:14), then to Jesus they essentially said, "Who made you the Christ?" The church leaders questioned Jesus' authority to cleanse the temple (John 2:18) and to teach there (Matthew 21:23). They claimed He actually was a servant of the devil (Matthew 12:22–32). When He hung dying, they heaped scorn upon him, saying, "If you are the Son of God, come down from the cross" (Matthew 27:40). All of this, however, was exactly as the prophets and Jesus had predicted. He said, "The Son of Man must suffer many things and be rejected by the elders and chief priests and scribes, and be killed, and on the third day be raised" (Luke 9:22). Rejection was built into the plan of salvation, and it was sketched out in the Old Testament stories of salvation.

From Divine Worship to Bovine Worship— The Golden Calf

Take the time to read through the entire sermon of Stephen in Acts 7. As you do, ask yourself what is "between the lines" in the sermon? What is his purpose in preaching this way? How is Stephen implicitly convicting the Jews throughout the sermon by using examples from Israel's past?

In the section above, we took a look at part of Stephen's speech to the Sanhedrin in Acts 7. Take the time to read through that whole sermon (7:1–53). At first glance, all Stephen appears to be doing is summarizing the history of the Old

Testament, from Abraham to Solomon. Then, at the conclusion, he seems unexpectedly to launch into an all-out verbal assault against his hearers for being a "stiff-necked people, uncircumcised in heart and ears, [who] always resist the Holy Spirit" (Acts 7:51).

Read the chapter a second time, however, and pay careful attention to how Stephen tells the story. His purpose is not simply to give facts and figures from Israel's past. He is casting his spotlight on certain incidents in the course of their history when the Israelites rejected the men God sent to them—a pattern of rejection that came to fulfillment when they "betrayed and murdered" the Righteous One, Jesus Christ (Acts 7:52). The whole sermon, therefore, and not merely the concluding section, is directed against those who, like their ancestors, rejected the servant of the Lord.

We will take a closer look at one section of Stephen's sermon in a moment. Before we do, read through Exodus 32 and answer these questions: What prompts the Israelites to ask Aaron to make a "god" for them? How does Aaron respond? Note Aaron's words in 32:4–5. How do his words suggest that the golden calf—while idolatrous—was actually intended to be symbol for the Lord? What does Moses do when he comes down from the mountain?

A key figure of rejection for Stephen is Moses (Acts 7:17–43). We have already highlighted one incident that Stephen highlighted also, that is, the initial rejection of Moses when he was forty years old. Now we'll move to another story—the Golden Calf (Exodus 32). First, we'll summarize what happened at Mt. Sinai, returning to Acts 7 to see how Stephen applies it to the Sanhedrin.

The long and short of the Golden Calf account is this: Israel wanted to worship God on their own terms, not God's. What really mattered to them was not what the Lord said but what they desired or dreamed worship should be. The nation had been at Mt. Sinai for a relatively short period of time when Moses ascended the mountain to receive the oracles of God (Exodus 24:15–18). During the forty days during which Moses was absent, the people grew

restless. They approached Aaron and demanded, "Up, make us gods who shall go before us. As for this Moses, the man who brought us up out of the land of Egypt, we do not know what has become of him" (Exodus 32:1).

Aaron seemed all eagerness. He collected gold from the people and with it crafted a golden calf. The people cheered, "'This is your god, O Israel, that brought you out of the land of Egypt!' So when Aaron saw it, he built an altar before it. And Aaron made a proclamation and said, 'Tomorrow is a feast to the Lord'" (Exodus 32:4–5 NKJV).

Judging by the people's words and Aaron's proclamation, the calf was intended to be a sort of visible symbol for Yahweh, not an idol or foreign god. Aaron does *not* say, "Tomorrow is a feast to this calf," but a "feast to the Lord," that is, Yaweh, the true God. But it did not matter what the intentions of Aaron or the people were: Yahweh never said He wanted a cow to be His icon! In fact, He strictly forbade any image to be made of Himself (Exodus 20:3–6). So this golden calf was in fact an idol. Whatever the people's intentions may have been, this icon was in fact an object of idolatry, for it falsely depicted the true God. Through their actions, Israel shifted from divine worship to idol worship!

Return to Acts 7 and reread verses 38–42. What did Moses give to the Israelites? How did they respond? Therefore, what did this failure of Israel ultimately originate from? What was the chief problem that leads to this evil result?

The fallout of this sin can be read about in Exodus 32:7–35. The people were chastised severely when Moses descended from the mountain, but he interceded for them, and the Lord only slew some of the wrongdoers. The calf was smashed to smithereens. This episode would go down in the history books of the nation as one of their biggest failures (see Deuteronomy 9:13–29; Psalm 106:19–23; Nehemiah 9:17–19). But from what did this failure originate? From ignorance? No. The golden calf was built because the people rejected the preaching of Moses, which was none other than the preaching of God.

Let's return to the sermon of Stephen to see how he relates this account. He says,

> [Moses] received living oracles to give to us. Our fathers refused to obey him, but thrust him aside, and in their heart they turned to Egypt, saying to Aaron, "Make for us gods who will go before us. As for this Moses who led us out from the land of Egypt, we do not know what has become of him." And they made a calf in those days, and offered a sacrifice to the idol and were rejoicing in the works of their hands. (Acts 7:38–41)

Stephen could not say it more clearly. Moses received the words of the Lord: "living oracles." But the Israelites turned a deaf ear to his preaching. Just as the bully "thrust him aside" when Moses tried to make peace in Egypt (Acts 7:27), so all the Israelites "thrust him aside" at Sinai (7:39). Same sad song, second verse. One might say that Moses took the Israelites out of Egypt, but he couldn't take Egypt out of the Israelites, for in their hearts they longed after the old ways. Refusing to listen to Moses and refusing Yahweh Himself, they turned toward the works of their own idolatrous hands.

Read Acts 7:51–52. In what way does this summarize the point that Stephen has been making all along? What parallel does Stephen draw between Jesus and the prophets of old? What connection does Jesus draw between Himself and Moses in John 5:39–47? According to these verses, why did the Jews reject Jesus?

When Stephen wrapped up his sermon, he made explicit what he had been strongly suggesting all along: "As your fathers did, so do you. Which of the prophets did not your fathers persecute? And they killed those who announced beforehand the coming of the Righteous One, whom you have now betrayed and murdered" (7:51–52). Just as the children of Israel made Moses into a suffering servant, so too the Messiah, whom Moses announced.

The rejection of the preaching of Moses was also a charge that Jesus Himself brought against the Jews of His generation. There is an added twist however. For Jesus says that in repudiating Him as the Christ, they are in fact scorning the preaching of Moses. First, He said to them, "You search the Scriptures because you think that in them you have eternal life; and it is they that bear witness about Me, yet you refuse to come to Me that you may have life," (John 5:39–40). Thus, the Bible—as a whole—points to and is all about Jesus. Then, our Lord narrows the focus to the writings and preaching of Moses: "Do not think that I will accuse you to the Father. There is one who accuses you: Moses, on whom you have set your hope. If you believed Moses, you would believe Me; for he wrote of Me. But if you do not believe his writings, how will you believe My words?" (John 5:45–47). There you have it! To thrust aside Moses means thrusting aside Jesus, and vice versa. If the Jews had not been so blind to the very writings they claimed to be so strongly committed to, they would have seen that Moses announced the coming of the Messiah—and that Messiah was standing before them.

The preaching of Jesus Himself, of course, was disdained by the multitudes. We have already pointed out what happened to Him in His first hometown sermon (Luke 4:16–30). After Jesus taught that His flesh and blood is the true manna from heaven, given for the life of the world, "many of His disciples turned back and no longer walked with Him" (John 6:66; see 6:22–65). Story after story in the Gospels reveals how many dismissed Jesus or outwardly hated Him because of what He taught. "Egypt" was just as much in the heart of Jesus' generation as that of Moses.

Consider these words from the explanation to the Third Commandment in the Small Catechism: "We should fear and love God so that we do not despise preaching and His Word, but hold it sacred and gladly hear and learn it" (p. 10). In what way are we also guilty of the sin of the Israelites in despising preaching and God's Word? Keep in mind that to despise does not necessarily mean to hate. To despise is to act as if God's Word is unimportant, as if we can live without it, as if it were not as crucial as God says it is.

Summarize what you have learned concern-

ing the parallels between Moses and Jesus. How are they similar, and how are they different? In what ways are they both "suffering servants" of the Lord?

Rather than pointing fingers at the Israelites of Moses' day or the time of Jesus, however, we need to examine our own hearts. How have we have despised the Word of God, treated it lightly, or outwardly repudiated it since it did not suit our taste or fit with our preconceived notions? For the same flesh and blood that rebelled against Moses and Jesus is wrapped around our bones and flowing through our veins. We are no different, and certainly no better. The message of repentance resounds in our ears just as it did in theirs.

But the message that Moses preached and Jesus embodied—as well as preached—is the same. The Father is "merciful and gracious, slow to anger, and abounding in steadfast love and faithfulness, keeping steadfast love for thousands, forgiving iniquity and transgression and sin" (Exodus 34:6–7). What Jesus suffered was for our salvation. He was rejected that we, in Him, might be accepted by our Father in heaven. He did keep His Father's Word; He kept it for us who break it. In Him we are perfect, for in His baptismal bath our sins are washed away. We are clean. We are forgiven. We are made whole and alive in Him.

Conclusion

The author of Hebrews begins his sermon with these words: "Long ago, at many times and in many ways, God spoke to our fathers by the prophets, but in these last days He has spoken to us by His Son" (1:1–2). One of the "many ways" God spoke to us by His prophets was in the sufferings they endured. Though many things can and should be learned from what they endured, paramount among these is that the Prophet, Jesus Christ, would suffer as well. The lives of the prophets, such as Moses, provide a preview of the life of our Lord. Because "Jesus Christ is the same yesterday and today and forever" (Hebrews 13:8), we should expect consistency in the ways in which He acts on behalf of His Church.

And, of course, that is what we find. He announces beforehand, through His prophets, what He will do (Amos 3:7). He announces this, however, not just with words but with deeds.

So it was with Moses. From his near-death experience as an infant, to the rebuff he suffered from Israel at the age of forty, through the countless times he had to bear their rejection, hatred, and threats—in all this, Moses was a suffering servant of God and of His Church. In all this, the Lord also shows us what the prophet like Moses will suffer (Deuteronomy 18:15). But our Lord's sufferings, unlike those of Moses, are for our salvation. He bore the cross we could not bear. He was rejected that we might find acceptance in His flesh and blood. Only in Him do we, along with Moses, reach the true promised land, where suffering will finally come to an end.

Closing Prayer

O God, whose glory it is always to have mercy, be gracious to all who have gone astray from Your ways and bring them again with penitent hearts and steadfast faith to embrace and hold fast the unchangeable truth of Your Word; through Jesus Christ, Your Son, our Lord, who lives and reigns with You and the Holy Spirit, one God, now and forever. Amen.

(Collect for Lent 3, *Lutheran Service Book*)

OUT OF EGYPT MOSES

Moses—Suffering Savior

What images spring to mind when the name *Moses* is mentioned? Are they positive or negative? What overall portrait of him stands out in your mind?

The life of Moses is easily divided into three forty-year segments. Until the age of forty, he lived in Egypt. From age forty to eighty, he lived in Midian with his father-in-law and family. And from age eighty to one hundred twenty he pastored the Israelite congregation. Think of the various offices and vocations Moses had during these 120 years. From what you recall of his life story, what are some major ways in which the Lord called him to bear a cross?

Infant Murder

Read **Exodus 1**. How did the Israelites prosper in Egypt for a time? What led to problems with Pharaoh? What was this Egyptian ruler worried about? He tried three different ways to slow down or decimate the Israelite population. What are these three, and did they succeed? Tertullian, a church father, once remarked that the blood of the martyrs is the seed of the Church. In what way would this apply to the Israelite situation as well?

Pharaoh and the Egyptians did these horrible things to the people of God. What did many of the Israelites likely think about God's concern (or lack of concern) over their predica-

ment? This persecution of the people of God was one of many persecutions of the Church that happened in the Scriptures (and, of course, that continue to happen today). Why does God allow His Church to endure such afflictions? Do we even know why? What would God have the Church do during such times?

Read **Exodus 2:1–10**. The mother of Moses tried to hide him for three months, we are told, because she saw that he was a "fine" child (**2:2**). Some translations say that she saw he was a "beautiful" child. Why does this seem like a strange reason for a mother to hide her child? The Hebrew word variously translated "beautiful" or "fine" is literally "good." This is the same word that occurs seven times in **Genesis 1** as "good" or "very good." Think of Moses in relation to the "good" in Genesis 1. How might this tell us something about God's future plans for this child? How does Moses fit into God's "good" plan for creation?

When the mother of Moses places him into the Nile, how do we see God's invisible hand at work? How does He providentially direct everything to work out for Moses?

Between his infancy and his fortieth year, where was Moses? In **Acts 7:22**, what does Stephen tell us Moses was doing during this first stage of his life? In what way would the skills acquired during these years have been of assistance to him in later years?

In **Exodus 2:11**, we are told that Moses went out to see "his people"? What does this tell us about Moses' knowledge of his background?

After Moses killed the Egyptian, he fled to Midian, where he remained for the next forty years, until he was eighty years old. **Exodus 2:15–4:20** describe Moses' flight to Midian, his marriage, his call from God to deliver Israel, and his return. Briefly review the events in this chapter.

There are several similarities between Moses and Jesus regarding what was done to them while they were infants. In fact, in Matthew's Gospel, he assumes that his readers know the story of **Exodus 1–4**, for he uses language from this account to describe what happened to Jesus. Read **Matthew 2**, note the parallels between these two infancy narratives, and comment on their significance.

Compare the two rulers: Herod and Pharaoh. What did they do, and what drove them to do what they did?

Israel was in captivity in Egypt when Moses was born. Under what kind of political and spiritual captivity was Israel when Jesus was born? Note **Luke 2:1** and **John 8:34**.

Compare Herod's slaughter of the children in Bethlehem with Pharaoh's attempt to eradicate the male children of the Israelites. What means did God employ to save both Moses and Jesus?

Jesus remained in Egypt with Mary and Joseph until when? Read **Matthew 2:19–20**. Compare these verses with **Exodus 4:19**. Note the similarities in the verses. By imitating Exodus,

Matthew wants you, a hearer of his Gospel, to think in a certain way about Jesus. What is this way? Why would he want you to think of Jesus as a sort of New Moses?

Rejected by the People He Came to Save

Who Do You Think You Are?— Rejected Right Away

Like Joseph and Jesus, Moses suffered rejection from his countrymen in many ways. Reflect upon how God does not let these rejections spoil His plans for the salvation of His people. What does this tell us about the character of the Lord and His will for sinful humanity?

Read again **Exodus 2:11–14**. Why does Moses kill the Egyptian? Does this appear to be legitimate? Why or why not?

Some have been critical of this action, claiming Moses was acting rashly. Read **Acts 7:23–28**. What does **verse 25** tell us about Moses' motivation and assumption when he killed the Egyptian? If Moses already knew that God had chosen him to deliver the Israelites, how does this affect our interpretation of his killing of the Egyptian?

Read **Exodus 2:14** and **Acts 7:26–29**. Compare these two accounts of the same incident. What does Stephen add in **Acts 7** that is not explicit in Exodus 2. The next day, what reaction do the Israelites have to Moses? How are the Israelites not only rejecting Moses, but God as well?

In what way is this initial rejection of Moses a preview of how they act toward him in the future? The Israelite essentially accuses Moses of planning murder against him. Read **Exodus 14:10–12**; **16:1–3**; **17:1–3**; **Numbers 20:2–13**; **21:1–9**. In what future contexts do you hear an echo of this initial accusation that Moses was a killer?

Look at other times when the leadership of Moses was questioned. Who opposed Moses, for instance, in **Numbers 12:1–16**? What happened in **Numbers 14:1–4**? Who opposed the leadership of Moses in **Numbers 16**? How do similar problems still emerge in the Church today?

The rejection of Moses and his call from God to be Israel's leader and deliverer was the same sort of rejection endured by Jesus as well. This should have come as no surprise to those who knew about the prophecies of the Messiah. What do these passages tell us about how the Messiah will or will not be received: **Psalm 118:22** (see **Matthew 21:42**) and **Isaiah 52:13–53:12**?

Moses was rejected on the first occasion in which he showed himself to be Israel's deliverer. What happened to Jesus when He publicly preached that He was the Deliverer sent from the Father (**Luke 4:16–30**)? How was the divine authority of Jesus questioned? See **John 2:18** and **Matthew 21:23**. Of what did they accuse Jesus in **Matthew 12:22–32**?

From Divine Worship to Bovine Worship— The Golden Calf

Take the time to read through the entire sermon of Stephen in **Acts 7**. As you do, ask yourself what is "between the lines" in the sermon? What is his purpose in preaching this way? How is he implicitly convicting the Jews throughout the sermon by using examples from Israel's past?

We will take a closer look at one section of Stephen's sermon in a moment (**7:17–43**). Before we do, read through **Exodus 32** and answer these questions: What prompts the

Israelites to ask Aaron to make a "god" for them? How does Aaron respond? Note Aaron's words in **32:4–5**. How do his words suggest that the golden calf—while idolatrous—was actually intended to be symbol for the Lord? What does Moses do when he comes down from the mountain?

Return to **Acts 7** and reread **verses 38–42**. What did Moses give to the Israelites? How did they respond? Therefore, what did this failure of Israel ultimately originate from? What was the chief problem that leads to this evil result?

Read **Acts 7:51–52**. In what way does this summarize the point that Stephen has been making all along? What parallel does Stephen draw between Jesus and the prophets of old? What connection does Jesus draw between Himself and Moses in **John 5:39–47**? According to these verses, why did the Jews reject Jesus?

Consider these words from the explanation to the Third Commandment in the Small Catechism: "We should fear and love God so that we do not despise preaching and His Word, but hold it sacred and gladly hear and learn it" (p. 10). In what way are we also guilty of the sin of the Israelites in despising preaching and God's Word? Keep in mind that to despise does not necessarily mean to hate. To despise is to act as if God's Word is unimportant, as if we can live without it, as if it were not as crucial as God says it is.

Summarize what you have learned concerning the parallels between Moses and Jesus. How are they similar, and how are they different? In what ways are they both "suffering servants" of the Lord?

4
SATAN'S TARGET
JOB

Opening Prayer

Almighty God, graciously behold this Your family for whom Lord Jesus Christ was willing to be betrayed and delivered into the hands of sinful men to suffer death upon the cross; through the same Jesus Christ, Your Son, our Lord, who lives and reigns with You and the Holy Spirit, one God, now and forever. Amen.

(Collect for Good Friday, *Lutheran Service Book*).

Job—Father, Husband, Priest, Sufferer

Discuss what you know about the story of Job. How does it compare with other stories of human tragedy and suffering? How is it similar and different?

Our world is awash in stories of human tragedy and suffering. From the atrocities of the Holocaust to the loss of life in natural disasters around the globe, examples aplenty exist of how dark and deadly the life we pass through is. Some who suffer tell their own stories or have their stories passed on by others; most, sadly, do not. Very few accounts that reach the ears of others come close to capturing in words the deepest depths of human woe. But one does—and does well—the story of Job.

Unlike Joseph and Moses, the sufferings of Job did not befall him because his family members hated him or his congregation closed their ears to his preaching. He faced down no earthly tyrants, nor did he spend time unjustly behind bars. His case was, in many ways, unique. Job's hardships originated in heaven—coming on the heels of a dialogue between the Lord and the devil concerning the righteousness of Job. The manifold troubles that Job endured stemmed from this encounter.

Although the Scriptures do not expressly inform us as to the epoch in which Job lived, there are several hints within his story that suggest a time prior to the life of Moses and the exodus from Egypt (i.e., prior to the fifteenth century BC). For example, the account is silent as to the existence of Israel. Also, Job lives not within Canaan but in the land of Uz. Most significantly, Job serves as a priest for his family, offering sacrifices on their behalf, as did the patri-

archs and other heads of families prior to the establishment of the priesthood of Aaron and his sons. Thus Job most likely lived well over fifteen hundred years prior to the birth of Jesus.

Though our focus will fall primarily upon the prose sections of Job (chapters 1–2 and 42), it is important to realize the vast majority of the book is an extensive poetic dialogue or debate between Job and his fair-weather friends concerning the reasons for his sufferings and how he should respond to them. Three of the friends—Eliphaz, Bildad, and Zophar—claim Job must be getting what he has coming to him for some awful skeleton he's hidden in his closet. Job protests—much too vehemently though—that he is innocent. If the divine Judge would only give him a day in court, he would strive to show that he has a clean record. After Job and the three friends are finally out of breath, Elihu speaks up, preaching truthfully both about man and God. In the end, the Lord censures Job and his comrades (except Elihu) for speaking wrongly or rashly concerning Him and the way He deals with humanity. The final chapter of the book describes how God

healed Job, commanded him to serve as a priest for his friends, and doubly restored what he had lost in the tragedies that befell him.

With Joseph, Moses, and many others, Job is ranked as one of many sufferings servants in the Scriptures. As we study the misfortunes he endured, as well as his response to them, we'll have a dual focus. First, as we have done in previous lessons, we'll relate these to the similar afflictions that were endured by the Messiah, showing how Job, too, served as an "image of God's Son" (as Luther called suffering Joseph). Second, we'll emphasize how the story of Job provides a primary lesson in what we call the "theology of the cross."

In the Crosshairs of Satan

Read Job 1. What picture is painted of Job in the opening verses? What characterizes him? What is the purpose of this description in the overall story?

The Book of Job begins with an introduction of the man himself. There is first of all a description of his piety: he was "blameless and upright, one who feared God and turned away from evil" (Job 1:1). The Old Testament used this language to sum up the life of a godly believer. This does not mean Job was perfect, without sin. Rather, it means he believed in God and strove diligently to live a life in conformity with the will of the Lord. And, as we'll soon discover, Job was exemplary in this life of piety, so exemplary in fact that God claimed none on earth could keep pace with His servant Job (Job 1:8).

What kinds of blessings had the Lord lavished upon Job? In addition to being a husband and father, what other important responsibility did Job have? See Job 1:5.

The Lord had loaded this saint down with blessings. In material possessions, Job's land was bulging with livestock; he was master to very many servants. Job was, in fact, "the greatest of the people in the east," the Rockefeller of his day. He had an extensive family as well—a wife, seven sons, and three daughters. These eleven he cared for not only as a husband and father, but also as a priest. This was a duty commonly performed by the head of the household prior to the establishment of the priesthood of Aaron. For every so often, after his children has gotten together for a family shindig, Job would "send and consecrate them, and he would rise early in the morning and offer burnt offerings according to the number of them all" (Job 1:5). So, all in all, we might say Job was pious, rich, and relatively trouble-free. He seemed to have everything going for him. Until . . .

Who are the "sons of God" who appear before the Lord in Job 1:6? How does the Lord describe Job to Satan? What does Satan claim is the reason that Job is upright? What does he claim Job will do if the Lord takes away what the Lord has given him? Satan is thus claiming that Job's faith is not really in the Lord but in what?

One day when the angels (here called "sons of God") were presenting themselves before the Lord, the fallen angel, Satan, also showed up. What followed was a discussion between God and the prince of hell concerning Job, as to how he would stand up under the pressure of intense suffering (Job 1:7–12). The devil claimed that God and Job had a sort of "you scratch my back and I'll scratch yours" agreement. God had made Job wealthy and protected him from harm so, in turn, Job trusted and worshiped the Lord. Rip that all away from him, Satan challenged, and Job will curse you to your face. With that, the Lord gave permission to the devil, more or less, to wreck Job's life. Only Job's own body was off-limits.

Review verses 12–19. What does Satan do to Job?

Thus begins Job's very own D-day. Four messengers in a row came to Job; with each the news grew progressively worse (Job 1:13–19). Thieves had stolen his oxen and donkeys and murdered his servants. Fire had fallen from heaven and burned up Job's sheep and shepherds. Raiders ran off with his camels and slew his servants watching them. Then the worse news came. During one of the family parties a tornado, or the like, demolished the house where the children of Job were feasting. Alas, all ten were confirmed dead.

Reflect upon Job's response to this tragedy. Bear in mind that Job is not privy to what we know; he is not aware of the dialogue in heaven between the devil and God. How did he react both verbally and nonverbally to these tragedies? What do each of his responses mean? What kind of confession of faith is Job making? Restate Job's response in other words. What does this tell us about how we should view all the gifts we have in this life?

At this point, Satan was no doubt licking his lips, waiting for the moment when Job would shake his fist at the heavens and curse God to his face. But the devil waited in vain. For rather than doing either, Job

Arose and tore his robe and shaved his head and fell on the ground and worshiped. And he said, "Naked I came from my mother's womb, and naked shall I return. The LORD gave, and the LORD has taken away; blessed be the name of the LORD." In all this Job did not sin or charge

God with wrong. (Job 1:20–22)

Instead of cursing God, Job, in his deep sorrow, humbles himself before God. Job's actions reflect his words. In all this tragedy, Job recognizes that all he had was a gift from God. As God's children, we too need to realize that all good things in our lives are blessings from our loving heavenly Father.

What are some wrong questions to ask about this story? What often drives the kinds of questions we ask in times of tragedy? For instance, do we not often assume that the evil that has befallen us or our loved one is "unfair" or "unjust"? Disuss how various questions reveal as much about what is wrong with us as what is wrong with the world in general.

A whole host of questions arise from this story (and those after it). For example: What was the devil doing in heaven in the first place? Whatever caused God to toss Job's name into the ring during this conversation? Why would the Lord allow Satan to inflict such harm and death? How could even the strongest saint refrain from sinning in the face of such indescribable heartache? The questions go on and on.

One very important point to bear in mind when asking such questions—and others like them—is that the Scriptures do not always give us answers to the questions we are most prone to ask. Or, if the Scriptures do supply us with answers, the replies will not always be intellectually satisfying. That is, the answer may not make sense to us; the divine response may not seem rational or fair or what we expect. Also, God may not explain everything we wonder about to us. Our most burning questions may be left unanswered.

What is fate? Does fate ever play a part in why sufferings befall people? If fate were real, what would that tell us about God's control of the world?

That being said, let us address, for now, these questions that Scripture does answer—questions that we ourselves should be asking: Why does God allow believers such as Job to suffer? Is there a pur-

pose behind all this? If so, what is it?

First, we must underline the fact that suffering is never due to fate. It was not bad luck that befell poor Job. Even though it does often seem that the world is chaotic, spinning out of control, those appearances are deceiving. The God who made the heavens and the earth has not abandoned that which He made—not at all! Our heavenly Father is in gracious control of history: the history of the cosmos, of countries, of families, and, yes, of every individual. The Lord is not watching creation "from a distance" but is rather intimately and purposefully involved in the nitty-gritty of what happens here.

This creation, however, is also a very fallen creation. That with which the Lord "works" is in very bad working condition. Evil exists and thrives, permeating every aspect of life. Because of the sin of man, creation itself has undergone transformation—a bad transformation—from what it once was. From world wars to mosquito bites, every painful aspect of this world can be traced back to the rebellion in Eden. So, yes, the Lord reigns over and directs the affairs of this world, but it is a world gone terribly wrong.

Luther once said that "everything that belongs to God must be crucified." How does this apply in the case of Job? Relate this to Matthew 16:24–25. What does it mean to take up one's cross? What does it mean to lose one's life and thus save it? What overall purpose do our crosses serve? Read Galatians 2:20.

Having said this, why did our good and gracious Father, who directs the course of events in this fallen world, let such sufferings hit Job? Luther's short answer is because "everything that belongs to God must be crucified." That means that all the children of the heavenly Father must bear their crosses with Jesus. As our Lord Himself said, "If anyone would come after Me, let him deny himself and take up his cross and follow Me" (Matthew 16:24). A Christian without a cross is a contradiction in terms. The purpose of this cross is twofold: death and life. As Jesus continues to say, "For whoever would save his life will lose it, but whoever loses his life for My sake will find it" (Matthew 16:25). Our crosses therefore slay us. We lose our life in them, for they crucify in us all reliance upon ourselves, our own works and wisdom. At the same time, while nailed to our crosses, we learn reliance upon God. Faith is born and nurtured when we realize that we cannot help ourselves, cannot save ourselves, but must look wholly to Him who supplies everything we need and everything we have. In losing our life, we gain the life of Christ, for "we live and move and have our being" in Him (Acts 17:28). Thus, with St. Paul we confess, "It is no longer I who live, but Christ who lives in me" (Galatians 2:20). Everything that belongs to God must be crucified, for in that way we are conformed to the image of the crucified Christ, receiving life in Him.

Job was living what is called the theology of the cross. This means that we view all of life as we view the cross. The only way we can truly know and confess what was happening on the cross is by the Word of God, not by sight or feelings. God's Word tells us who was on the cross (God Himself) and what was being done on the cross (salvation for all humanity). Thus, what is real often appears under the guise of its opposite. Apply this theology to the following examples:

* Holy Baptism: Contrast what human eyes see taking place in Baptism with what the Word of God tells us is really taking place.

* Holy Communion: Contrast what the eyes see and the mouth tastes in Holy Communion with what the Word tells us is actually consumed.

* Job's sufferings: Contrast what appeared to be happening to Job with what the Word of God tells us. For instance, did it appear as if God loved Job or hated him? Did it appear as if the Lord was gracious and merciful or the opposite?

* Our sufferings: Apply the theology of the cross to your own trials and tribulations.

So Job, too, had to be "crucified." The purpose behind his sufferings was death and life. Job was learning—more every passing day—what is meant by the *theology of the cross*. By this "cross theology" we mean that the way in which God deals with each one of us is revealed in the crucifixion of Jesus. Consider this: no person looking at our Lord on the cross would have seen God in the flesh, the King of kings, reigning from the tree in glory. Instead, what would they have observed? A tortured "criminal" stripped naked, gasping for breath, dripping with blood, slowly dying in this merciless form of execution. That is all the naked eye would have beheld. It takes an eye clothed with the Word of God to see what and who was really there. Thus, the divine Word frequently opposes human perception. What we see, experience, and feel is often directly contrary to what God promises, affirms, and gives. We live by His Word, which is to say, we live by faith. Faith is "the assurance of things hoped for, the conviction of things not seen" (Hebrews 11:1).

The theology of the cross applies to the whole life of a Christian. For instance, in the dark moments of my life, I may not feel that Christ loves me; in fact, I might feel like God has become my worst enemy! But in His Word, Christ says He does love me, no matter what. So I believe He does. That is, I live by faith in His Word, not my emotions.

The theology of the cross applies to the Sacraments as well. When I am baptized, the experience may not leave me feeling born again, adopted by the heavenly Father, forgiven, and renewed. But the Word of God says all these things happen, so I believe they do. Similarly, when I receive the Lord's Supper, the bread doesn't taste like Christ's flesh, nor does the wine taste like His blood. But I do not live by the taste in my mouth, but by every Word that proceeds from the mouth of God! What God's Word says, that *is* reality. What I feel, think, and experience may very well be unreality. As one pastor put it, we must "look through our ears" to see what God is doing for us and in us, that is, we must look from the perspective of what our ears hear from God's Word. We can rely on that speech, without fail, for God cannot lie.

Thus Job was a living example of the theology of the cross. From the perspective of fallen man, Job had every right to conclude that God hated him . . . if there even was a God. Job's emotions would have tempted him to give up the faith, curse God, and resign himself to a life of despair and sorrow. That is what Satan was betting on. But despite the intense affliction he was enduring, Job held fast to the Word of God. He knew that "the LORD gave" him everything he had (Job 1:21): livestock, servants, children—everything. Job also knew that God could take them back, which He had done. Job came into the world with nothing but his "birthday suit" and he would leave this world with nothing more. No one drags a U-haul to heaven. Every gift received in this life comes from God. So Job confessed that the Lord is gracious and merciful, abounding in love, as His Word says He is.

Compare Job's response to his tragedies with the response of Jesus to His sufferings. For instance, compare their relative "innocence" and uprightness. What did they say regarding God in their most intense sufferings (Job 1:20–22 and Matthew 26:36–42)?

"In all this Job did not sin or charge God with wrong" (Job 1:22). Here we observe one aspect of the kinship between Job as a suffering servant and the Suffering Servant, Jesus Christ. In spite of the fact that Job had just been "crucified," the cross he now bore did not press him into sinning or blaming God. Indeed, he did the exact opposite! Job "fell on the ground and worshiped" (Job 1:20), confessed that the Lord is gracious, and blessed the divine name. Though the wolves of doubt howled all around this tormented lamb, he listened to the voice of the divine Shepherd, who promised, "I will never leave you, nor will I ever forsake you. I love you. You are mine. Doubt not. I am with you always" (see Hebrews 13:5 and Matthew 28:20).

So it was also in the Passion of our Lord. When the incredible weight of this world's sin, as well as divine wrath against that sin bore down upon Him, He did not sin or blame God. Rather, Christ "fell on His face and prayed" (Matthew 26:39). Yes, even when He cried from the cross, "My God, My God, why have You forsaken Me" (Mark 15:34; see also Psalm 22:1), Jesus continued to trust in His Father, for He lived by faith in the Word of God. As Jesus replied to the devil after His first temptation, "Man shall not live by bread alone, but by every word that comes from the mouth of God" (Matthew 4:4). As a true man (as well as true God), Christ clung steadfastly to the promises of His Father. He confessed, as did Job, that the Father is loving and merciful. He believed that truth in the face of what He endured, not only on the cross but during every trial and tribulation He faced. Though the "crucifixion" of Job was quite different from that of Jesus, and the reasons were different, one thing that unites them is their confession and life of faith.

In the Crosshairs of Satan, Again

Read Job 2:1–10. Compare the first conversation of God and Satan with this one. What does God confirm regarding Job's reaction in the first round of attacks? What does the devil claim will finally get Job to curse God? What does Satan do to this one who has already suffered so much?

Contrast Job's life now with all the blessings described in the first few verses of the book. What things have been reversed?

Though Job underwent all the miseries connected with the demise of his children and the murder of his servants, as well as the theft of possessions, his suffering was far from over. Indeed, his "crucifixion" had only just begun. For, as the second chapter of the book informs us, "Again there was a day when the sons of God came to present themselves before the LORD, and Satan also came among them to present himself before the LORD" (Job 2:1). As they had before, God and Satan entered into a dialogue that quickly focused upon Job. The Lord said, "Have you considered My servant Job, that there is none like him on the earth, a blameless and upright man, who fears God and turns away from evil? He still holds fast his integrity, although you incited Me against him to destroy him without reason" (Job 2:3).

With these words, the Lord underscores the fact that in the first round of attacks, Job did not do what Satan had expected him to do. No curse against God exited Job's lips. Instead, he uttered a humble confession of the power and goodness of the Creator. Job held fast his integrity, feared God, and turned away from evil.

No doubt anticipating this point, Satan comes prepared with a response and with another challenge. He is ready for round two. And this time, he supposes, he is sure to win. The devil answers, "Skin for skin! All that a man has he will give for his life. But stretch out Your hand and touch his bone and his flesh, and he will curse You to Your face" (Job 2:4–5).

In other words, Satan argues, the only reason Job hasn't cursed God yet is because his body is still untouched. Everything Job lost was outside his own person. But attack his own body and he's sure to rail against the heavens. As before, the Lord then allows Satan to assail Job—this time his body—but with a qualification: "Behold he is in your hand; only spare his life" (Job 2:6).

The devil, we are told, took full advantage of the permission granted him, sparing no part of Job. For he "struck Job with loathsome sores from the sole of his foot to the crown of his head. And [Job] took a piece of broken pottery with which to scrape himself while he sat in the ashes" (Job 2:7–8). Pause for a moment to compare this painful depiction of the believer with the happy picture given in Job 1:1–5. Virtually everything has been reversed, hasn't it? From riches to rags, health to horror, a man with everything to a man with nothing.

How does Job's wife react to this second round of suffering? How would you characterize her reaction? In what ways are she and Job different? How can our friends or loved ones actually worsen our sufferings by what they say to us in response to our trials?

Well, almost nothing—Job does still have his wife, but, as we hear, even she seems to have been transformed into a weapon in Satan's hand. For Mrs. Job, viewing her husband's misery—and, of course,

suffering untold grief herself—tempts him to throw in the towel. She asks, "Do you still hold fast your integrity? Curse God and die" (Job 2:9). One might suggest that with a wife like this, who needs enemies? Her bitter, blunt words serve as a reminder of a distressing but very true fact: sufferers are very often rejected by those whose love they most desire and need. Friends forget them; parents or siblings shun them; church members ignore them. Their pain is, of course, compounded by this unloving treatment. Certainly, if Job ever needed the support and love of his wife, it was now. How her encouragement would have strengthened him! But, instead, she chides, "Give it up! What are you waiting for? Curse God and die!"

How does Job respond to his wife? What does he encourage her to do?

Job's response to his wife is not what one might expect. He does not lash out at her, nor remain silent. His answer is both a loving corrective and a confession of his continuing trust in God: "You speak as one of the foolish women would speak. Shall we receive good from God, and shall we not receive evil?" The writer then adds, "In all this Job did not sin with his lips" (Job 2:10). Job attempts to pull his wife out of the chasm of despair into which she evidently tumbled. To her, Job is saying, "My dear wife, let us not forget the good things that the Lord lavished upon us in years gone by. He gave us seven sons and three daughters. And though they are not with us now, they are with their Father in heaven and we shall see them again. He made us wealthy. He gave us our health. We lacked nothing. All this we had as a gift from God. We did not earn or deserve it. He gave it to us because He loved us. Now He has taken it away. But remember, He has not taken us away from Himself. Though we must now receive evil from God, He Himself is not evil. The cross we bear now, we shall not bear forever."

In this second round of sufferings, Job continued to exemplify what it means to live the theology of the cross. How incessantly the devil must have tempted him to scowl upward at the face of the God who had "clearly" become his foe! How many curses Satan must have planted in the mind of Job that he could have launched heavenward! But as before, all is in vain. Defying every temptation, Job keeps on living not by what he feels or experiences but by what the Father told him in His Word. His emotions may growl, "God hates you," but the Word promises, "God loves you." His heart may yell, "The Lord has forsaken you," but the Word affirms, "God will never leave you, never forsake you." Job knows that everything that belongs to God must be crucified. The cross he bears may kill him, but in Christ he lives on.

Job trusted in the Lord despite the heavy crosses he was bearing. However, his faith was not a generic faith in a generic deity but trust in the gracious Lord who promised to send His Son to win salvation for sinful humanity. Job had faith in the Messiah, the Anointed One. Read Genesis 3:15 as one example of the promise of the coming Seed who would gain victory for us. Read also Job 19:23–27 as Job's own confession of faith in the Messiah. How does he describe the work of his Redeemer?

That last statement is important and deserves more explanation—in Christ, Job lives on. One might ask, How could Job trust in Christ? Didn't he live more than fifteen hundred years before the birth of Jesus? Like all believers who lived before the incarnation, Job did not have faith in a generic deity—not even a generic deity who was good, loving, and forgiving. He believed in the promised Messiah, the Son of the Father, who would one day come in the flesh to redeem Job, and all humankind, from sin and death. Beginning with the days of Adam, time and again, the Lord promised His people that He would send such a Savior. Indeed, immediately after the transgression of our first parents, the Lord spoke what is often called the "Protoevangelium," that is, the "First Gospel." Addressing the devil, the Lord said, "I will put enmity Between you and the woman, And between your seed and her Seed; He shall bruise your head And you shall bruise His heel'" (Genesis 3:15 NKJV). The Seed or Offspring of the woman would come to "bruise" the head of the satanic serpent. That is, He would destroy the power of him who brought sin into the world. At the same time, however, as His heel crushed the serpent's head, the fangs of the viper would pierce His heel and inject their deadly venom. So it happened in the crucifixion of Jesus. He "bruised" the devil's head, but in so doing, He Himself was killed. His death, however, freed all of us Adams and Eves from the power of sin, death, and hell. The promise was fulfilled by the Seed of the woman, the Son born of the Virgin Mary.

Promises such as this one were repeated and expanded throughout the history of the kingdom of God in the Old Testament. Job certainly knew them. He believed and confessed them to be true. He looked forward in faith to the day when the Seed would be born and undo the hellish doing of the satanic snake. Indeed, Job himself confesses his trust in the Messiah in a well-known passage from later in the book. He says,

"Oh that my words were written! Oh that they were inscribed in a book! Oh that with an iron pen and lead they were engraved in the rock forever! For I know that my Redeemer lives, and at the last He will stand upon the earth. And after my skin has been thus destroyed, yet in my flesh I shall see God, whom I shall see for myself, and my eyes shall behold, and not another. My heart faints within me!" (Job 19:23–27)

The Church echoes these words of Job every time she sings "I Know that My Redeemer Lives" (*Lutheran Worship* 264; *The Lutheran Hymnal* 200). This Easter and funeral hymn is based on this bold confession of the Messiah. Job knows and believes that his Redeemer is alive, that He will come to stand upon the earth as a flesh-and-blood man. Job himself, after his skin has been destroyed, will be resurrected so that in his own perfected flesh he shall see the God who redeemed him. What a bold confession! It clearly testifies to the faith Job had in the Messiah—a faith shared by all those in the Old Testament who looked forward in hope to the advent of the promised Seed.

The "Comforting" Friends of Job

Read Job 2:11–13. Why do the three friends visit Job? What is their reaction upon seeing him? What does this tell us about the magnitude of his suffering?

We do not know how long Job remained in the horrid physical condition described in Job 2:7–8. It could have been weeks, months, or even years. In any case, sometime after this evil came upon Job, word got around to three of his friends—Eliphaz, Bildad, and Zophar—regarding what transpired. These acquaintances "made an appointment together to come and show [Job] sympathy and comfort him" (2:11). Their friend was so disfigured, however, that at first they didn't even recognize him (2:12)! Deeply grieved over his condition, they sat down with him on the ground for a whole week, no one uttering a word, "for they saw that his suffering was very great" (2:13).

As one reads the story of Job from chapter 3 onward, Job's responses change remarkably from his earlier confessions. Read through samples of these in Job 3–29. For instance, summarize Job's lament in chapter 3. What does he wish for in 3:16? What vivid image does he employ in 6:4? What does Job plead for in 23:1–7?

It is at this point in the narrative that the tenor of Job's statements changes substantially. Evidently, as the pain and heartache of his condition continued or even increased, Job failed to maintain such positive responses to the disasters as he initially uttered (Job 1:20–21; 2:10). In chapter 3, he curses the day of his birth, wishing that he would have expired when he left the womb (v. 11) or been stillborn (v. 16), so that he might have escaped the suffering he was now forced to endure. He depicts himself as a target for the divine archer, who pierced his body with poisonous arrows (6:4). He longs for a "day in court," when he could present his case before the celestial Judge, plead his innocence, and be acquitted (23:1–7). Time and again, Job vents his frustration, anger, pain, doubt, and grief, often calling into question the justice of the Almighty.

What kind of battle is waging inside Job? How does Paul describe this battle in Romans 7? How can the fact that this tug-of-war happened inside a saint such as Job be of comfort to us? What does it reveal about our condition and divine compassion and patience?

Most people who have read through the entire Book of Job marvel at the vast difference between Job's opening confessions of trust in God and his subsequent laments or outbursts against the unfairness of what he is enduring. This, however, should really come as no surprise. Especially when bearing the heaviest crosses, the day-to-day existence of believers is very much like a yo-yo, up and down, from faith to doubt, from hope to despair. This happens because of the war being waged within the Christian between the "old man" and the "new man," as Paul terms them (Ephesians 4:22–24 NKJV; Colossians 3:9–10 NKJV). The "old man," that is, the sinful nature rooted within us, hates God, does not trust Him, and lives as a willing pawn of the devil. The "new man," re-created in the image of Christ Himself, is the exact opposite. The believer, having both these "men" or "natures," lives in an unceasing state of battle. So it was for Job, he speaks according to the "new man" in the opening two chapters of the book, but frequently in the poetic dialogues that follow, Job's words bear witness to the tug-of-war going on within him between "Job as sinner" and "Job as saint."

There is some comfort for us in this. For if vacillation between hope and despair, faith and doubt, happened within the heart and mind of Job yet the Lord sustained and loved him through his ups and downs, then certainly God will do the same for us as well. The Lord is patient and forgiving. He surely does not approve of doubt and despair—indeed, he rebukes it—but He also remembers that we are "but flesh, a wind that passes and comes not again" (Psalm 78:39). The Lord is well aware that we are weak, sinful creatures who all too easily give way to the temptations of the flesh. In His compassion, our heavenly Father sustains us in our times of weakness, as an earthly father does his children. Thus, as the Lord did for this "super-saint," so He does for us. We walk not alone through the valley of the shadow of death, for our Good Shepherd strides alongside us.

What was the purpose of the visit of the friends of Job according to Job 2:11? But what does Job say concerning them in Job 16:2? For a summary of their primary message to Job, read Job 4:7–9. What is Eliphaz saying? Of what is he accusing Job? Describe the theology of Job's friends. Were they judging Job's situation according to faith or sight?

Now back to Job's friends. What are we to say of them? Though they supposedly came "to show him sympathy and comfort him" (Job 2:12), one searches in vain for such manifestations of love in their speeches to him. At one point Job grumbles, "Miserable comforters are you all" (16:2). What one finds, with ever-increasing ferocity, is a direct verbal attack upon the sufferer. In the first recorded speech, given by Eliphaz, he sums up the incessant argument of the three, "Remember: who that was innocent ever perished? Or where were the upright cut off? As I have seen, those who plow iniquity and sow trouble reap the same. By the breath of God they perish, and by the blast of His anger they are consumed" (4:7–9). In other words, "Job, you're gettin' what you got comin' to you." Time and time again, the friends imply that Job is keeping some deep, dark secret sin hidden in his conscience that he needs to confess. Because Job has not confessed, God launched this all-out attack against him. Thus, according to the friends, Job is reaping what he has sown. They leave no room for the possibility that Job is suffering for any other reason. Job is being punished by the Almighty. Case closed!

With what kind of theology are these friends working? The direct opposite of the theology of the cross, this is called the "theology of glory." *Cross theology* confesses that God cannot be truly known by mere reflection upon what you see with your eyes, much less what you feel in your heart. You must give heed to the Word of God. *Glory theology*, on the other hand, holds that God is truly known in matters of the senses. For example, if I am pleasing to God, this will be reflected in how well I do in life.

Material success, happiness, good health, and so forth are signs that I must be acceptable to the Lord. The theology of glory says sufferings, poverty, poor health, and the like show that I must not be pleasing to God. While cross theology says what *is* by means of what the ears hear from God's Word, glory theology says what *is* by means of what the eyes see or the heart feels or the head thinks.

Job's friends are theologians of glory, through and through. They view his loss of family, wealth, and health as a sure sign that God has turned against Job because Job turned against God. They live not by faith but sight. Their eyes tell them what is true, not God's Word. Thus they accuse Job so vehemently, convinced that he is a hypocrite. Otherwise, why would God have allowed such tragedies to befall him?

Compare the false theology and accusations of Job's friends with what the enemies of Jesus said to Him while He hung on the cross. See, for example, Luke 23:39 and Matthew 27:39–43. What assumptions about those who are suffering do these accusations have in common?

Do we not hear in the words of Job's "friends" an echo of the words hurled at our Savior as He hung from the cross? All around the place of crucifixion stood "theologians of glory." The one criminal railed at him, "Are you not the Christ? Save yourself and us!" (Luke 23:39). Those who passed by made fun of him, shaking their heads and mocking, "You who would destroy the temple and rebuild it in three days, save Yourself! If You are the Son of God, come down from the cross" (Matthew 27:40).

Christ's primary enemies: the chief priests, scribes, and elders of the Jews likewise scoffed, "He saved others; He cannot save Himself. He is the King of Israel; let Him come down now from the cross, and we will believe in Him. He trusts in God; let God deliver Him now, if He desires Him. For He said, 'I am the Son of God'" (Matthew 27:41–43). All who maligned Jesus believed the same thing: the sufferings He was enduring were proof positive that He was not who He claimed to be—the Messiah.

They believed that what they saw told them the truth, the whole truth, and nothing but the truth. Jesus was not the Messiah; it was as plain as the nose on their face. These adversaries and mockers lived not by the Word of God but by what they took in with their five senses. Like the friends of Job, they thought they could discern from the external situation of the sufferer how He stood in relation to God. This is the theology of glory, the theology incessantly preached by the devil himself.

We mentioned earlier that sufferers are often abandoned by those they need the most during their times of trial and tribulation. Here, too, we see the life of our Lord mirrored in the life of Job. Job's wife and friends abandon him—not physically, of course, for they are still there. Rather, their abandonment takes a far worse form. They abandon hope for him. They abandon encouragement, prayer, and love. While he is undergoing his "crucifixion," they sting him with words that only accuse or tempt him to despair. Like Job, our Lord could not count on His friends to give Him comfort or encouragement during His hardest trials. One of His disciples, Judas Iscariot, sells Him out for thirty pieces of silver (Matthew 26:47–50). When Jesus is arrested in the Garden of Gethsemane, "all the disciples left Him and fled" (Matthew 26:56), as He Himself had predicted (Matthew 26:30–35). While Jesus is being dragged from one court to another, his disciple Simon Peter denies three times that he knows who Jesus is—the third time throwing in curses for good measure (Matthew 26:69–75). As it was with Job, so it was with our Lord. While bearing the weight of their respective crosses, they went without the help and support of friends. God alone was their refuge and strength.

Job—Restored and Blessed

In the last few chapters of Job, the Lord Himself speaks (chapters 38–41). He declares, in short, that He is God and His ways are beyond human comprehension. He does not, nor ever will, "make sense" to us—at least, in the way we think of sense. In response to these divine speeches, twice Job repents (40:3–5; 42:1–6). What is Job repenting of? How had he thought and spoken wrongly concerning God? What does this teach us about how to respond to tragedy and suffering?

People often complain that life is "not fair." If fairness, however, means getting what you have coming to you—good or bad—then do we really want God to be fair with us? What do we say in the Confession of sins in the Divine Service regarding what we have deserved? See page 158 of *Lutheran Worship* and page 16 of *The Lutheran Hymnal*. Apply this to Job as well. Though Job was not being punished for a "big sin" he had committed, did he have any right to complain that God was not being just and fair with him? Why or why not?

Now we skip ahead to the end of the Book of Job. And what an end it is! From the deepest depths of human pain and suffering, Job emerges by divine grace to a new life overflowing with blessings. After his own crucifixion (multiple ones!), Job is raised from the dead, as it were. Just as the beginning of the story taught every believer about life under the cross, so the end of the story is a vivid testimony of life after the cross.

Throughout the debates between Job and his friends, it became clear that none of them were completely free from blame. The faults of the friends—their "theology of glory" and their accusatory speeches—have been sufficiently covered earlier. For his part, Job protested his innocence too much. Though he certainly was not being punished for some particular transgression(s), nevertheless, he, like all sinners, deserved worse. In short, he deserved hell. But he did not get hell. Let no one even think of saying he suffered hellish pain. The truth is there is no such thing as "hell on earth." Hell is hell. Nothing comes close to hell on this side of the grave. Indeed, to a person truly in hell, the darkest day of Job's suffering would have seemed like a day in paradise. Job went through untold horrors, yes, but by divine grace he was spared everlasting punishment.

In the last few chapters of Job (38–41), the Lord chides His servant, for Job "darkens counsel by words without knowledge" (38:2). In several speeches, God proclaims that He alone is wise, He alone is the one who created and sustains the world, and He alone is the one who knows what is best for man. Finally, when God has stepped down from His pulpit, Job voices his "Amen" to the preaching by admitting that he "uttered what [he] did not understand" (42:3). He repents "in dust and ashes" (42:6).

Read Job 42:7–9. In what way had Job spoken rightly concerning God but his friends spoken wrongly? Discuss what this divine judgment tells us about the importance of teaching rightly about the Word of God.

What does God instruct Job to do? What is the Lord's response? Discuss what this tells us about the way the Lord deals with humanity.

But from those "dust and ashes" the Lord raises him up, heals him, and restores him. In 42:7–9, God takes Job's friends to task, for they did not speak rightly of Him, as did His servant Job. For unlike his friends, Job acknowledged his sin, his lack of understanding, his repentance, and his faith in God. To speak rightly of God is to say "Amen" to what God first says. And that "Amen" Job had confessed.

As at the beginning of the story, when Job had served as priest for his wife and children, so now as his friends offer sacrifices, he prays on their behalf. In the context of sacrificial blood, Job speaks intercessory prayers toward the throne of grace to ask pardon for the "folly" of his friends (42:8). And that pardon is granted for "the LORD accepted Job's prayer" (42:9).

Read 42:10–17. What did the Lord do for Job? Note that the number of sheep, camels, oxen, and donkeys owned by Job were all doubled (compare with Job 1:3). Why is Job not given double the amount of children?

In the remaining verses, Job's full restoration—indeed, double restoration—is described. "The LORD gave Job twice as much as he had before" (42:10)

and "blessed the latter days of Job more than his beginning" (42:12). For instance, the Lord blesses him with twice as many livestock as before. But what about his children? If he had seven sons and three daughters in the beginning (1:2), why is he only given "seven sons and three daughters" in his restoration (42:13)? Why not fourteen sons and six daughters? The implied answer is this: Because Job did not "lose" his first ten children in the same way he truly lost his livestock. Those ten children were with their heavenly Father. They had not ceased to exist but had only been taken to their everlasting home. The Lord really gave Job twenty children: ten with him on earth and ten awaiting him in heaven.

There is a reflection in this final chapter of the work of our great High Priest, Jesus Christ. Discuss the following points as you compare them:

* Job's friends offer sacrifices. Why was sacrifice—in particular, the blood of sacrifices—so important in the Old Testament? See Leviticus 17:11. In what way was blood a gift of God to His Church?

* Contrasts Hebrews 10:4 with Leviticus 4:20, 26, 31, 35? What two seemingly contradictory things are said about animal blood and its relation to forgiveness? To solve the apparent contradiction, think of animal blood as an element of creation in an Old Testament sacrament, like water in Baptism or bread and wine in the Lord's Supper. How does this answer the question?

* Very often Jesus' death for us is described as a sacrifice. See Isaiah 53:10; John 1:29; Romans 8:3; Ephesians 5:2; and Hebrews 9:11–14. What relationship is there between the sacrifices of the Old Testament—like those offered by Job—and the sacrifice of Jesus Himself? How does knowledge of this relationship help to deepen our knowledge of the significance of what Job does for his friends?

* One of the chief duties of the priest was to pray for the people. This is what Job the priest

does for his friends in Job 42:8–9. In what way does our great High Priest pray for us? See Romans 8:34.

The Christian reader, who always holds the image of Jesus before the pages of Scripture, sees a certain reflection of our Lord Jesus in this final chapter of Job. In the restoration of Job, his priestly sacrifices, and his intercessory prayer, we observe a parallel to the person and work of our resurrected great High Priest. To understand how, we need to grasp the theological significance of priests and sacrifices before the birth of Jesus.

In the Old Testament, the blood of sacrifices was not a gift to God; rather, the blood was God's gift to people—sinful people, who needed cleansing and forgiveness. The Lord makes this clear in the Book of Leviticus: "For the life of the flesh is in the blood, and I have given it for you on the altar to make atonement for your souls, for it is the blood that makes atonement by the life" (17:11). The blood is a gracious, divine gift. But, in and of itself, animal blood could not bestow forgiveness any more than other elements of creation such as bread or wine or water. As the writer of Hebrews says, "For it is impossible for the blood of bulls and goats to take away sins" (10:4).

But if animal blood could not convey forgiveness, why does Scripture state several times that if a believer offers this or that sacrifice "he shall be forgiven" (e.g., Leviticus 4:20, 26, 31, 35; 5:10, 13, 16, 18)? The answer can be supplied in a way similar to the way the catechism answers the question about how the water in Baptism can do "such great things" (p. 22). We might say it like this:

How can animal blood do such great things? Answer: Certainly not just animal blood, but the Word of God in and with the blood does these things, along with the faith which trusts this Word of God in the blood. For without God's Word, the blood is plain animal blood and no sacrifice, but with the Word of God, it is a sacrifice that bestows forgiveness.

The Lord instituted these sacrifices for Israel, just as He instituted Baptism and the Lord's Supper for the Church. His word of promise, of forgiveness, was attached to them. They convey forgiveness to the believer but only by virtue of the future atonement of Christ, just as our Sacraments convey forgiveness only because of the past atonement of Christ. Note this well: The sacrifice of Jesus has been and is truly the only atoning sacrifice that has ever been offered. These Old Testament animal sacrifices pointed ahead to that future atoning sacrifice of "the Lamb of God, who takes away the sin of the world" (John 1:29).

In addition to this, the priests who offered these sacrifices bore an office that pointed ahead to the office of the Messiah, whom both the Psalms (110:4) and the Book of Hebrews call a "priest" (4:14–16). The Old Testament priests both represented God to the people and the people to God. As the representatives of the people before God, they prayed for God's people in the temple. As the representatives of God to the people, they proclaimed His Word, pronounced His benediction, and handled the flesh and blood of the sacrifices. Thus, both priests and sacrifices pointed ahead to the office and work of the Messiah. They sketched in pencil what He would fill with color.

Job's service as a priest for his friends by interceding for them provides a picture of the Messiah. The sacrifices they offered truly conveyed forgiveness to Job's friends, for they were offered in view of the sacrifice of "the Lamb of God, who takes away the sin of the world" (John 1:29). Job as priest bears the office that will finally be filled by One who comes as the High Priest who is able "to sympathize with our weaknesses . . . who in every respect has been tempted as we are, yet without sin" (Hebrews 4:15). As Job interceded for Eliphaz, Bildad, and Zophar, so Jesus "is at the right hand of God, who indeed is interceding for us" (Romans 8:34).

Conclusion

We thank God that the story of the suffering servant Job was recorded for posterity. How many believers have profited from his story! How many other suffering servants of Christ have drawn strength from hearing of how the Lord sustained Job in the valley of the shadow of evil and death! In the Book of Job, we see one of the clearest examples in all Scripture of the theology of the cross. In Job's sufferings, we learn what it means to live by faith in the Word of God. We learn what it means to say "No!" to emotions and experiences that would turn us away from Christ, and to say "Yes!" to His Word alone. We also see the pattern of the Messiah Himself in the sufferings and eventual exaltation of this servant of God. When viewed in light of the cross and resurrection of our Lord, the story of Job becomes more than just the story of one man's woes. It also echoes the woes of the one man Jesus Christ, who suffered more greatly than Job did, was killed, and literally rose from the dead. All this He did for Job's salvation and for ours. Thanks be to Him!

Closing Prayer

O God, Protector of all who trust in You, without whom nothing is strong and nothing is holy, multiply Your mercy on us that, with You as our ruler and guide, we may so pass through things temporal that we lose not the things eternal; through Jesus Christ, Your Son, our Lord, who lives and reigns with You and the Holy Spirit, one God, now and forever. Amen.

(Collect for Trinity 3, *Lutheran Service Book*)

SATAN'S TARGET JOB

Job—Father, Husband, Priest, Sufferer

Discuss what you know about the story of Job. How does it compare with other stories of human tragedy and suffering? How is it similar and different?

In the Crosshairs of Satan

Read **Job 1**. What picture is painted of Job in the opening verses? What characterizes him? What is the purpose of this description in the overall story?

What kinds of blessings had the Lord lavished upon Job? In addition to being a husband and father, what other important responsibility did Job have? See **Job 1:5**.

Who are the "sons of God" who appear before the Lord in **Job 1:6**? How does the Lord describe Job to Satan? What does Satan claim is the reason that Job is upright? What does he claim Job will do if the Lord takes away what the Lord has given him? Satan is thus claiming that Job's faith is not really in the Lord but in what?

Review **verses 12–19**. What does Satan do to Job?

Reflect upon Job's response to this tragedy. Bear in mind that Job is not privy to what we know; he is not aware of the dialogue in heaven between the devil and God. How did he react both verbally and nonverbally to these tragedies? What do each of his responses mean? What kind of confession of faith is Job making? Restate Job's response in other words. What does this tell us about how we should view all the gifts we have in this life?

What are some wrong questions to ask about this story? What often drives the kinds of questions we ask in times of tragedy? For instance, do we not often assume that the evil that has befallen us or our loved one is "unfair" or "unjust"? Discuss how various questions reveal as much about what is wrong with us as what is wrong with the world in general.

What is fate? Does fate ever play a part in why sufferings befall people? If fate were real, what would that tell us about God's control of the world?

Luther once said that "everything that belongs to God must be crucified." How does this apply in the case of Job? Relate this to **Matthew 16:24–25**. What does it mean to take up one's cross? What does it mean to lose one's life and thus save it? What overall purpose do our crosses serve? Read **Galatians 2:20**.

Job was living what is called the theology of the cross. This means that we view all of life as we view the cross. The only way we can truly know and confess what was happening on the cross is by the Word of God, not by sight or feelings. God's Word tells us who was on the cross (God Himself) and what was being done on the cross (salvation for all humanity). Thus, what is real often appears under the guise of its opposite. Apply this theology to the following examples:

* Holy Baptism: Contrast what human eyes see taking place in Baptism with what the Word of God tells us is really taking place.

* Holy Communion: Contrast what the eyes see and the mouth tastes in Holy Communion with what the Word tells us is actually consumed.

* Job's sufferings: Contrast what appeared to be happening to Job with what the Word of God tells us. For instance, did it appear as if God loved Job or hated him? Did it appear as if the Lord was gracious and merciful or the opposite?

* Our sufferings: Apply the theology of the cross to your own trials and tribulations.

Compare Job's response to his tragedies with the response of Jesus to His sufferings. For instance, compare their relative "innocence" and uprightness. What did they say regarding God in their most intense sufferings (**Job 1:20–22** and **Matthew 26:36–42**)?

In the Crosshairs of Satan, Again

Read **Job 2:1–10**. Compare the first conversation of God and Satan with this one. What does God confirm regarding Job's reaction in the first round of attacks? What does the devil claim will finally get Job to curse God? What does Satan do to this one who has already suffered so much?

Contrast Job's life now with all the blessings described in the first few verses of the book. What things have been reversed?

How does Job's wife react to this second round of suffering? How would you characterize her reaction? In what ways are she and Job different? How can our friends or loved ones actually worsen our sufferings by what they say to us in response to our trials?

How does Job respond to his wife? What does he encourage her to do?

Job trusted in the Lord despite the heavy crosses he was bearing. However, his faith was not a generic faith in a generic deity but trust in the gracious Lord who promised to send His Son to win salvation for sinful humanity. Job had faith in the Messiah, the Anointed One. Read **Genesis 3:15** as one example of the promise of the coming Seed who would gain victory for us. Read also **Job 19:23–27** as Job's own confession of faith in the Messiah. How does he describe the work of his Redeemer?

The "Comforting" Friends of Job

Read **Job 2:11–13**. Why do the three friends visit Job? What is their reaction upon seeing him? What does this tell us about the magnitude of his suffering?

As one reads the story of Job from chapter 3 onward, Job's responses change remarkably from his earlier confessions. Read through samples of these in **Job 3–29**. For instance, summarize Job's lament in chapter 3. What does he wish for in **3:16**? What vivid image does he employ in **6:4**? What does Job plead for in **23:1–7**?

What kind of battle is waging inside Job? How does Paul describe this battle in Romans 7? How can the fact that this tug-of-war happened inside a saint such as Job be of comfort to us? What does it reveal about our condition and divine compassion and patience?

What was the purpose of the visit of the friends of Job according to **Job 2:11**? But what does Job say concerning them in **Job 16:2**? For a summary of their primary message to Job, read **Job 4:7–9**. What is Eliphaz saying? Of what is he accusing Job? Describe the theology of Job's friends. Were they judging Job's situation according to faith or sight?

Compare the false theology and accusations of Job's friends with what the enemies of Jesus said to Him while He hung on the cross. See, for example, **Luke 23:39** and **Matthew 27:39–43**. What assumptions about those who are suffering do these accusations have in common?

Job—Restored and Blessed

In the last few chapters of Job, the Lord Himself speaks (**chapters 38–41**). He declares, in short, that He is God and His ways are beyond human comprehension. He does not, nor ever will, "make sense" to us—at least, in the way we think of sense. In response to these divine speeches, twice Job repents (**40:3–5**; **42:1–6**). What is Job repenting of? How had he thought and spoken wrongly concerning God? What does this teach us about how to respond to tragedy and suffering?

People often complain that life is "not fair." If fairness, however, means getting what you have coming to you—good or bad—then do we really want God to be fair with us? What do we say in the Confession of sins in the Divine Service regarding what we have deserved? See page 158 of *Lutheran Worship* and page 16 of *The Lutheran Hymnal*. Apply this to Job as well. Though Job was not being punished for a "big sin" he had committed, did he have any right to complain that God was not being just and fair with him? Why or why not?

Read **42:7–9**. In what way had Job spoken rightly concerning God but his friends spoken wrongly? Discuss what this divine judgment tells us about the importance of teaching rightly about the Word of God.

What does God instruct Job to do? What is the Lord's response? Discuss what this tells us about the way the Lord deals with humanity.

Read **Job 42:10–17**. What did the Lord do for Job? Note that the number of sheep, camels, oxen, and donkeys owned by Job were all doubled (compare with **Job 1:3**). Why is Job not given double the number of children?

There is a reflection in this final chapter of the work of our great High Priest, Jesus Christ. Discuss the following points as you compare them:

* Job's friends offer sacrifices. Why was sacrifice—in particular, the blood of sacrifices—so important in the Old Testament? See **Leviticus 17:11**. In what way was blood a gift of God to His Church?

* Contrast **Hebrews 10:4** with **Leviticus 4:20, 26, 31, 35**? What two seemingly contradictory things are said about animal blood and its relation to forgiveness? To solve the apparent contradiction, think of animal blood as an element of creation in an Old Testament sacrament, like water in Baptism or bread and wine in the Lord's Supper. How does this answer the question?

* Very often Jesus' death for us is described as a sacrifice. See **Isaiah 53:10**; **John 1:29**; **Romans 8:3**; **Ephesians 5:2**; and **Hebrews 9:11–14**. What relationship is there between the sacrifices of the Old Testament—like those offered by Job—and the sacrifice of Jesus Himself? How does knowledge of this relationship help to deepen our knowledge of the significance of what Job does for his friends?

* One of the chief duties of the priest was to pray for the people. This is what Job the priest does for his friends in **Job 42:8–9**. In what way does our great High Priest pray for us. See **Romans 8:34**.

CHOSEN LEADER DAVID

Prayer

Merciful Lord, cleanse and defend Your Church by the sacrifice of Christ. United with Him in Holy Baptism, give us grace to receive with thanksgiving the fruits of His redeeming work and daily follow in His way; through the same Jesus Christ, Your Son, our Lord, who lives and reigns with You and the Holy Spirit, one God, now and forever. Amen

(Collect for Proper 15, *Lutheran Service Book*).

Introduction

We often think of biblical persons in pairs, such as Adam and Eve. What are some other pairs of biblical characters that spring to mind? What names would associate most closely with David?

Take a moment to review the life of David. Perhaps in the introduction to a study Bible you can find a survey of the events in 1–2 Samuel, the books that document David's deeds and misdeeds. Acquaint yourself with the major events in his life.

In everyday speech, as well as in biblical stories, we naturally tend to lump together the names of certain people. Some names just seem to fit hand in glove. For instance, we normally speak of those joined in holy wedlock as one unit: Adam and Eve or Abraham and Sarah. Oftentimes, we also put two brothers together, such as Cain and Abel or Jacob and Esau. Sometimes we even place the names of enemies side by side: Moses and Pharaoh or David and Goliath.

The joining of such names usually brings with it a certain story, or stories, associated with them. For example, the mention of David and Goliath takes our mind to the battle scene where young David outfitted with five pebbles faces down and takes out the titanic warrior who's armed to the teeth.

Though perhaps David's fame is most closely associated with this victory in his teenage years, this was but a minor incident on his way up the regal ladder that finally landed him on the throne of Israel. Over the course of his lifetime, David's name would be closely linked with the names of many others, some enemies (David and Saul), some illicit lovers

(David and Bathsheba), and some backstabbers (David and Ahithophel). A few of these people are better known than others (you might be asking, "Ahitho-who?"), but every one of them impacted the life of David in some way, for better or for worse. Very often, as we shall see, it was, by far, for worse.

In this lesson, we're going to bypass the more famous—and infamous—parts of David's life, such as when he went head-to-head with Goliath or had his adulterous rendezvous with Bathsheba. Instead, we'll devote most of our time to those parts of his biography where David was undergoing "crucifixion" as he bore the crosses of persecution and betrayal. We'll chiefly observe two truths. First, that David, in his sufferings, served as a personal preview of the suffering Son of David. Thus, he, like Joseph, Moses, and Job, served as an "image of God's Son" (Luther). Second—and here is David's uniqueness— we'll learn that the same psalms that David prayed while enduring his crosses were psalms very much at home on the lips of Jesus as well. Indeed, these psalms, although written and prayed by David during his trials, fit the tribulations of our Lord more exactly than those of their original author.

Not only was David a king and warrior, he was also a poet. Look through the Book of Psalms and notice how many times David's name appears in the heading of the psalm. What else is sometimes described in these headings? See, for instance, Psalms 3; 18; 51; 56; and 59. What profit might there be in reading these psalms alongside the historical events that gave rise to them? What might they show us?

Our overarching goal in this lesson, as throughout these studies, is to illustrate what Jesus meant when He claimed that all the Scriptures speak of Him (Luke 24:27, 44; John 5:36, 46). Jesus is the be-all and the end-all of the Bible, from Genesis through Revelation, no portion excluded. Christ was foretold in prophecies and even revealed Himself visually at times, for instance, in the form of the Angel of the Lord (Exodus 3:1). But Christ was also foreshadowed in the lives of men such as David, whose deeds and vocations reflected the pattern filled and fulfilled by Jesus. Thus, as we now study David, let us look at him through the lens of the One called David's Son.

"Saul, Saul, Why Do You Persecute Me?" David and Saul

Saul was the first king of Israel. Though he began his reign well, things soon went sour. Read through 1 Samuel 13:1–15 and 1 Samuel 15 for examples of his wrongdoing. Note especially 15:28. What does the prophet Samuel tell Saul the Lord will do? How do you suppose this affected Saul? What would he begin to do?

David was secretly anointed king in 1 Samuel 16, but, of course, Saul was unaware of this. Trace the events through which Saul became acquainted with David? You'll find these in 1 Samuel 16:14–18:5. In this initial stage, what did Saul think of David? How would you characterize their relationship?

David's story begins in 1 Samuel 16 when the prophet Samuel (secretly) anointed the youngest son of Jesse as the next king of Israel. Though Saul currently occupied the throne, the Lord had a rapidly growing list of grievances against him. For instance, when Samuel was running behind time to conduct a prebattle sacrifice, Saul evidently suffered with the proverbial ants in his pants (1 Samuel 13:1–15). So Saul took it upon himself to offer the sacrifice—a major no-no of biblical law. When Samuel showed up—catching Saul red-handed—the king whitewashed his actions by claiming he had "forced himself" to do it (v. 12). No fool, Samuel stated in no uncertain terms that this overtly rebellious act signaled that Saul would have no dynasty; the Lord would seek a man after His own heart.

On a later occasion, when Saul and his soldiers were given very precise instructions to slaughter all the people and all the beasts of the enemy, they spared the king and the best of the livestock (1 Samuel 15). Once more, when Samuel arrived on the scene, Saul went through a creative song and dance about why he decided not to stick to the letter of

the law. This was the last straw. The prophet lambasted the king for his sinful behavior and informed him that the Lord had torn the kingdom away from him to give to Saul's neighbor. This anonymous neighbor, as we learn in 1 Samuel 16, was young David.

It wasn't long before Saul began to realize that David was the "neighbor" whom Samuel said would replace Saul (15:28). Read 1 Samuel 18:6–9. What sparked the friction between the two men? What emotions were driving Saul?

Given this background, it comes as no surprise that King Saul was keeping his eyes peeled for who this "neighbor" might be. Woe to that man if Saul could get his hands on him! When Saul first makes David's acquaintance, no red flags go up. David was, after all, just a teenage musician at the time 1 Samuel 16:14–23), not an experienced warrior or a suave politician—or so it seemed. Only after David slew Goliath (1 Samuel 17), and especially after the ladies began singing louder praises of David's military prowess than Saul's (1 Samuel 18:6–9), did the king put two and two together. "This must be the one," Saul surmised. So began the long, drawn-out history of Saul's attempt to eradicate his would-be successor to the crown.

A Window of Escape

The rest of 1 Samuel describes the many and various way in which Saul persecuted David. We will only examine a couple of them. The first deals with David's family. Read the following verses to understand how closely knit David was to the family of Saul: 1 Samuel 18:1–4 and 18:17–30. What kind of relationships did he have with Saul's children?

Our story is found in 1 Samuel 19:11–18. As background to Saul's murderous actions, read 1 Samuel 18:10–11; 18:25; 19:1; and 19:10. Through what efforts had Saul already tried to send David to an early grave?

Virtually the rest of the Book of 1 Samuel (18:10–31:13) documents the many and varied ways in which Saul and his henchmen conducted their persecution. It is not our intention to describe all of these; readers can check them out for themselves. What we want to do is highlight a couple of them for these reasons: (1) they are representative of ways in which the sufferings of this servant are akin to those of our Lord and (2) they provided the occasion for David to compose a psalm about the event.

The first of these incidents reveals just how far Saul was willing to go in order kill David (1 Samuel 19:11–18). To appreciate Saul's actions, recall that David was a mere servant of Saul, closely knit to the king's family. David not only forged a very close friendship with Jonathan, Saul's son (1 Samuel 18:1–4), but also he married Michal, Saul's daughter (1 Samuel 18:17–30). So David was not just hounded by "the king," the king was his own father-in-law!

Before the story we're about to study occurred, Saul had already revealed his devilish intent. Twice Saul tried to skewer David to the wall with his spear (1 Samuel 18:10–11; 19:10); once he attempted to get the Philistines to kill him (1 Samuel 18:25). Later, Saul commanded his servants to slay David (1 Samuel 19:1). Needless to say, David knew he had to stay on his toes if he expected to grow old and gray.

Read 1 Samuel 19:11–18. Describe the actions and attitudes of the various characters in the story. How does this account highlight the determination of Saul to murder his rival?

In 1 Samuel 19:11–18, we read that Saul sent messengers to David's house to keep an eye on him overnight. The plan evidently called for Saul to make the next day David's last. The scheme was foiled, however, when Michal found out her father was about to turn her into a widow. Under cover of darkness, she lowered David through a window, and he fled out of harm's way. Then, showing she had inherited some of her father's crafty ways, Michal put what amounted to a mannequin in the bed where her husband should have been sleeping. As the sun rose and the messengers came knocking, she reported that David was under the weather. Not willing to let that stop him, however, Saul demand-

ed, "Bring him up to me in the bed, that I may kill him," (1 Samuel 19:15). Now that's determination! When the bed was toted in, voila! There was the dummy, but no David. More than a little hot under the collar, Saul vented his rage at his daughter, who outfoxed her father yet again with a "little white lie" concerning how David got away.

You might wonder what was going through David's mind on this night of danger and escape. Some of these questions are answered by reading Psalm 59. Note the superscription of the psalm. As you read through the psalm, describe how David interprets this event. What are the key themes in this psalm? How does David speak of God and his enemies? What does he expect the Lord to be and to do for him?

As you read this story, you might wonder: What exactly was going through David's mind as all this transpired? Was he angry, scared, poker faced? How did David view his enemies and their diabolical actions? Questions such as these are at least partially answered by reading this account from 1 Samuel in synch with Psalm 59. Why? We are informed that this hymn or prayer was written "when Saul sent men to watch his house in order to kill him" (Psalm 59 superscription). This psalm provides a window into David's heart and mind.

Some key themes arise from this psalm. First, David knows that deliverance from his enemies lies completely in the hands of God (Psalm 59:1–2, 8–10, 16–17). Second, he has done nothing against those who seek his life (vv. 3–4). Third, David's enemies behave like wild dogs; they give no thought to the fact that God may be against them (vv. 6–7, 14–15). Fourth, the adversaries will be destroyed by the judgment of God (vv. 8, 11–14). Woven throughout these verses is David's confession that God is his fortress, strength, shield, king, love, and refuge. No matter what Saul and his other adversaries might try, David remains certain that God is on his side and will surely deliver him.

Consider the connection this event in David's life has to the life of Jesus. To aid you, read through the psalm again, this time thinking of

Christic as the one who prays these words. How do they fit with the life and sufferings of our Lord? How are David's words just as fitting—indeed, even more so—on the lips of Jesus?

Consider also the historic incident behind this psalm in the light of what happened to Jesus. Relate the actions of David's enemies to what the enemies of Jesus did to Him in these verses: Mark 3:2; Luke 14:1; 20:20; John 5:18; 7:1; 11:53. The Lord rescued David; how did Christ similarly escape from His foes? See John 8:59 and 11:54.

Keeping in mind both David's escape from attempted murder and the psalm he composed in response to that event, consider the following: What connection might this have to the life of our Lord Jesus? What kind of parallels do we see reflected in the sufferings of David and those of Christ?

First of all, remember something that ought to go without saying but that is worth stating explicitly nonetheless: Jesus prayed Psalm 59. How do we know this? Like every Israelite, Jesus grew up with the Book of Psalms as His "hymnal." In every synagogue service He attended, psalms were chanted. These hymns would have resounded in His every visit to the temple in Jerusalem. In Israelite homes, these same sacred songs were on the lips of the faithful. Thus, the prayer of David was also the prayer of Jesus, as it is for every believer.

More than that, however, this prayer especially fits the life of our Lord, for He, too, was surrounded by bloodthirsty men. Why did they seek His life? "For no transgression or sin of [His] . . . for not fault of [His], they run and make ready" (Psalm 59:3). They hounded Him wherever He went, as these doglike men pursued David (Psalm 59:6–7, 14–15). But Christ knew and confessed that His Father was His Strength and Shield and Refuge. Try what they might, the enemies could not ultimately defeat Him. For even from the grave, the Father vindicated His Son by resurrecting Him. Therefore, what David prayed was also rightly prayed by the Lord and Son of David. Indeed, Jesus still prays this psalm in and with His body, the Church, as His members suffer

persecutions.

Consider also the fact that the historic incident behind this psalm may easily be compared to similar happenings in the life of Jesus. Saul sent men to watch for David. So also, Jesus was constantly under the scrutiny of His adversaries. They watched Jesus so they could accuse Him (Mark 3:2; Luke 14:1); they sent spies to try and catch Him in a statement (Luke 20:20); they looked for opportunities to kill Him (John 5:18; 7:1; 11:53). As David escaped his enemies' evil schemes, so also Jesus frequently had to hide Himself to escape His enemies' murderous plots. When they tried to stone Jesus in the temple, He hid Himself (John 8:59). When they sought to kill Him, He stayed near the wilderness, away from their gaze and out of their grasp (John 11:54). The Lord had plans for both these suffering servants, and no evil ploys of men would thwart His goals for them. David would reign from his throne in Jerusalem, while Jesus would reign from the cross in Jerusalem.

David the Madman

The next incident is admittedly a rather bizarre one. Read 1 Samuel 21:10–15. Bearing in mind that Gath was a city filled with David's enemies, the Philistines, how might they interpret his actions? Why did he do what he did? What was the result?

The incident in David's life recorded in 1 Samuel 21:10–15 is admittedly rather strange. When it became abundantly clear that Saul would stop at nothing to assassinate David, the young man began to meander from place to place, seeking refuge wherever it presented itself. On one occasion, David hid out in the Philistine city of Gath. The king ruling this town was known both as Achish (his personal name) and Abimelech (a common "throne name"). The servants of Achish were more than a little suspicious of this Israelite refugee. Indeed, having recognized David, they informed their ruler that this man was "the king of the land" whose wartime exploits were famously lauded in Israelite chants (v. 11). When David realized his cover was blown, he set in motion an ingenious but bizarre escape plan. "He changed his behavior before them and pretended to be insane in their hands and made marks on the doors of the gate and let his spittle run down his beard" (v. 13).

Quite the plan, indeed, but it worked! The king of Gath, wholly bamboozled by David, remarked that he stood in no need of an extra madman hanging about his courts (1 Samuel 21:14–15). Taking advantage of his successful ruse, David escaped from this would-be tomb and took up residence in his next hideout, the cave of Adullam (1 Samuel 22:1).

David also composed a song or prayer after this incident: Psalm 34. Read through the psalm. What is the main message of this prayer? What are some of its primary themes?

As with the earlier episode of the "window escape," so here also David composed a poetic prayer to offer up in his time of need: Psalm 34. Given the precarious context that led to its composition, the main theme, quite appropriately, is that God rescues His people from all the dire straits in which they find themselves. Verse 19 captures the theme of the psalm: "Many are the afflictions of the righteous, but the LORD delivers him out of them all" (Psalm 34:19).

The verse following this one serves as a verbal bridge between this unusual incident in the life of David and one in the life of Jesus. David prayed: "He keeps all His bones, not one of them is broken" (Psalm 34:20).

Keeping in mind Psalm 34:20, read John 19:31–37. In 19:36, John says these things happened to fulfill the Scriptures. To which Scriptures is John referring? In 19:36, John likely has two verses in mind: Exodus 12:46 and Psalm 34:20. What is the Exodus passage about? What connection does the New Testament draw between the Passover lamb and Jesus? See John 1:36 and 1 Corinthians 5:7. Compare also the verse in the psalm with what happened to Jesus on the cross. How does this fit both the suffering of David in Gath and the suffering of Jesus on the cross? Read Psalm 34 anew, in light of the crucifixion of

Jesus. How does this open up a new understanding of the psalm? Which words seem especially appropriate when heard as prayed by our Savior?

In the Gospel of John, when the evangelist records the death of Jesus, he reports that the soldiers did not break His legs, as they did those of the two criminals who were executed alongside Him (19:31–33). Instead, the Roman pierced His side with a spear, resulting in the outflow of blood and water. "For these things took place," John informs us, "that the Scripture might be fulfilled, 'Not one of His bones will be broken'" (19:36).

What Scripture does John have in mind? It is likely twofold. First, he identifies Jesus as the true and final Passover Lamb. In Exodus 12, when the Lord instructs Moses regarding the Passover lambs, He commands, "You shall not break any of its bones" (Exodus 12:46). Since Jesus is the true Passover Lamb (John 1:36; 1 Corinthians 5:7), His bones also remain whole.

The second Scripture that John refers to is Psalm 34:20, the hymn David composed when he escaped from Gath. So, not only is Jesus the true and final Passover Lamb, He is also the true "righteous" man (Psalm 34:19) whose bones are not shattered by the Roman soldiers. Thus, the fact that our Lord's bones are left unbroken fulfills both Exodus 12 and Psalm 34.

Exodus 12:46
You shall not break any of its bones.

Psalm 34:20
He keeps all His bones; not one of them is broken.

John 19:36
Not one of His bones will be broken.

By quoting Psalm 34, John reveals that this hymn, which originated from the Lord's protection of David in Gath, received its fulfillment in the Lord's protection of Jesus in death. This protection, guaranteed (as it were) in the preservation of His bones on the cross, would be fully revealed three days later when the Father raised His Son, bones and flesh, from the Gath-like sepulcher. Therefore, though "many are the afflictions of the righteous, . . . the LORD delivers Him out of them all" (Psalm 34:19), even the ultimate affliction of death!

We learn from this psalm that in the life of David, even the most peculiar of incidents, such as his mock insanity, are viewed in light of the work of the Messiah. The history of David includes far more than mere history; it serves as an account that reveals how the Lord saves His anointed one(s) from destruction. When threatened by a foreign king and his servants, both David and the Son of David placed their confidence in the God of salvation, who heard their petitions and worked deliverance for them.

David Betrayed

David's sufferings did not end when he finally assumed the throne as king of Israel (2 Samuel 2:1–4 and 5:1–5). In many ways they increased! Survey the events narrated in 2 Samuel. What were some of the lowest points in David's reign? With which group of people did most of his sufferings originate?

The road David traveled from the day that Samuel secretly anointed him king of Israel (1 Samuel 16) to his public anointing and reception as the leader of the tribe of Judah (2 Samuel 2:1–4) and later king of all Israel (2 Samuel 5:1–5) was long and hard. Though bearing many crosses of persecution upon his back, this suffering servant proved faithful to his Lord.

The "crucifixion" of David, however, did not end when he took his seat on the throne of Israel. Indeed, in some ways, his sufferings accelerated. A quick survey of 2 Samuel readily demonstrates this. There was marital strife with Michal (6:16–23). David's affair with Bathsheba led to the death of their son (11:1–12:23). David's son Amnon raped his half sister Tamar (13:1–22). Another of David's sons, Absalom, Tamar's full brother, murdered Amnon in revenge for the rape (13:23–33). Absalom fled, then later returned, only to begin a conspiracy against his father, David (13:34–15:12). Absalom initiated a coup against David and seized control of Jerusalem, forcing his father to flee for his life (15:13–37). Later, David's men put Absalom to death, causing David great heartache (18:1–15). A man named Sheba led a rebellion against David that had to be squelched (20:1–22). The king conducted an unlawful census of Israel that angered God and led to the death of seventy thousand men in a plague (24:1–25). And, finally, when the king was on his last legs, his son Adonijah proclaimed himself king instead of Solomon, to whom David promised the crown (1 Kings 1:1–53). With such a life of strife and warfare, one can easily understand why David would begin one of his psalms with the cry, "O LORD, how many are my foes!" (Psalm 3:1). How many indeed!

As we did in the earlier section, so here we will focus our attention upon a couple of these stories, or specific incidents in these bigger narratives. Again, our goal is twofold: First, to demonstrate the kinship between David and Jesus in their respective sufferings as servants of the Father. Second, to take a look at psalms David wrote in response to these events and to show how David's prayers are also the prayers of our Lord.

Ahithophel: David's "Judas Iscariot"

The events we're about to study took place during Absalom's rebellion. To acquaint yourself with Absalom and his past, skim 2 Samuel 13–18. Answer the following: Who was Absalom in relation to David? Why did Absalom have to flee Jerusalem? What did he do when he returned? What evil did he perpetrate against the king? How did he die?

Some of the most heartrending trials that David endured were those that arose during Absalom's rebellion (2 Samuel 14–18). After murdering his half brother Amnon in retaliation for Amnon's rape of Tamar, Absalom's sister, this son of David fled into exile for many years. Upon his return, he began a systematic plan to steal away the hearts of his father's subjects. For four years he glad-handed the citizens of Israel, earning their favor, and turning them against the king (2 Samuel 15:1–7). Then, with a band of soldiers, Absalom prepared to enter

Jerusalem and seize control. When David and his subjects heard about the approaching coup, they took flight, leaving Jerusalem easy picking for Absalom and his cronies. As they left, however, not all David's subjects tagged along. A few of them, sensing a political opportunity, became turncoats, remaining behind to join with Absalom against their ruler. Most infamous among these was Ahithophel.

One of the men who rebelled against David during Absalom's coup was Ahithophel. How highly esteemed was this counselor of David (2 Samuel 16:23)? What did he do when Absalom asked him to join in the rebellion (2 Samuel 15:12)? What did David pray concerning Ahithophel (2 Samuel 15:31)?

Ahithophel was one of David's closest, wisest, most trusted advisors. It is said of him: "Now in those days the counsel which Ahithophel gave was as if one consulted the oracle of God; so was all the counsel of Ahithophel esteemed, both by David and by Absalom" (2 Samuel 16:23). When Absalom asked Ahithophel to join in the rebellion, this supposedly devoted servant of the king all too readily defected to the side of David's enemy son (2 Samuel 15:12). When the king heard of his treachery, he prayed that God would turn the counsel of Ahithophel into foolishness (2 Samuel 15:31). What David asked for was exactly what Absalom received.

Absalom asked advice from two men: Ahithophel and Hushai. What counsel did Ahithophel give (2 Samuel 17:1–4)? Given his past record (2 Samuel 16:23), what reaction did he likely expect when he urged the leader to do such and such? What counsel did Hushai give (2 Samuel 17:5–14)? Whose advice did Absalom follow? Why did it turn out this way?

Once Absalom took over the capital city, his next major decision was what to do about his father. He consulted two former advisors to the king: Ahithophel and Hushai (17:1–14). Ahithophel urged that twelve thousand soldiers be sent immediately into the wilderness to hunt down and kill King David. At first, this advice seemed good to Absalom. But

then they summoned Hushai—who, unbeknownst to them, was an undercover agent from David (2 Samuel 15:32–37). Hushai argued that Absalom should first summon men from all Israel, then take these warriors into battle, with himself—Absalom—leading them (2 Samuel 17:5–14). Having heard both plans, Absalom and his men decided in favor of Hushai's counsel. This happened, we are told, according to divine providence, for the Lord decided to bring evil upon Absalom (2 Samuel 17:14).

How did Ahithophel respond to the rejection of his counsel (2 Samuel 17:23)? Why? What drove him to do this?

The rejection of his plan was evidently too much for Ahithophel to bear. Accustomed to men heeding his advice as if it came from God Himself, and utterly dejected, he skulked away from the palace, "saddled his donkey and went off home to his own city" (2 Samuel 17:23). But he did not go home merely to pout and sulk. No, he had far worse plans. When he arrived, "he set his house in order and hanged himself, and he died and was buried in the tomb of his father" (v. 23). Ahithophel's suicide set his infamy in stone. Throughout all generations, he is remembered as the traitor of God's anointed king.

Although there is no superscription in Psalm 41 that confirms it was written during Absalom's rebellion, the content strongly suggests it was. Read through the psalm. How did David's adversaries treat him? How does David respond? What in particular does David say about his enemy in Psalm 41:9?

How is Ahithophel like Judas Iscariot, who betrayed Jesus? In what kind of relationship did they stand with their leader? What did each do to sell out his master? Moreover, compare how the two men ended their lives. Read 2 Samuel 17:23 and Matthew 27:5.

Not surprisingly, such a major event in the life of David prompted him to compose more than one psalm or prayer related to it. One of them, Psalm 3, we shall look at more closely in the section following this one. For now, we want to direct our attention to Psalm 41, which, judging from its content, strongly suggests that it also was composed during Absalom's uprising.

In Psalm 41, David describes the various ways in which his enemies desired and planned evil against him. In particular, they take advantage of his weakness to spread lies about him. They maliciously inquire, "When will he die and his name perish?" (v. 5). They slanderously report, "A deadly thing is poured out on him; he will not rise again from where he lies" (v. 8). These adversaries, however, are not faceless strangers, for David laments, "Even my close friend in whom I trusted, who ate my bread, has lifted his heel against me" (v. 9).

Such difficulties notwithstanding, David confesses his faith that the Lord will protect him, sustain him, and restore him. He also pleads, "O Lord, be gracious to me; heal me, for I have sinned against You!" (Psalm 41:4). Of all the periods in David's life, the rebellion of Absalom seems to fit best with the theme of this psalm, especially the reference to the "close friend" who has "lifted his heel" against the king. This "close friend" would be Ahithophel, who turned out to be David's own "Judas Iscariot."

The comparison of Ahithophel and Judas is very fitting for more than one reason. To begin with, Jesus quotes a verse from Psalm 41 in the context of the Passover meal with His disciples on the night when Judas sold Him out. In the Gospel of John, we read that Jesus, having washed His disciples' feet, speaks of the one in their company who is yet unclean. He goes on to explain:

> I am not speaking of all of you; I know whom I have chosen. But the Scripture will be fulfilled, "He who ate my bread has lifted his heel against me." I am telling you this now, before it takes place, that when it does take place you may believe that I am He. (John 13:18–19)

The one who is unclean, who ate bread with Jesus but also lifted up his heel against Him, was Judas. Thus, as David prayed this psalm with Ahithophel in mind, so Jesus prayed it in reference to Judas. The second connection between the two relates to the fact for which they are infamous: they both were traitors against the Lord's anointed. The

third parallel between Ahithophel and Judas—and one that very strongly argues for a connection between them—is that not only did they both commit suicide, they took their own life by the same method: hanging themselves. Ahithophel put his house in order, then "hanged himself" (2 Samuel 17:23), while Judas went out and "hanged himself" (Matthew 27:5).

Read John 13:18–19. What is the context in which Jesus says these words? What psalm does He quote? Note that as David prays this with Ahithophel in mind, Jesus prays it with Judas in mind.

Jesus' quotation of David's psalm, along with the parallels between the deeds and deaths of their respective betrayers, reveals certain similarities in their lives. The life of David and the life of Jesus are, as it were, laid one on top of the other, to be viewed as a composite whole. Just as David prayed this prayer in the midst of dire afflictions, so does our Lord, for on the very next day He will reach the peak of His sufferings. The gifts for which David beseeches the Lord in Psalm 41 were sought by Jesus also: protection, help, life, blessing. Moreover, as the adversaries of David willed and plotted his murder, so did the various foes of the Messiah.

How does the rest of Psalm 41 fit the life and sufferings of both David and the Son of David? Note that in Psalm 41:4, David confesses his own sin. If this prayer is prayed by the Messiah, how could He confess sins? Answer this question in light of 2 Corinthians 5:21 and Galatians 3:13. Whose sin is Jesus actually confessing?

One might object to the attribution of David's confession of sins in Psalm 41 to Jesus (Psalm 41:4). After all, you might ask, how could the Sinless One confess, "Heal me, for I have sinned against You"? The answer is actually quite simple. The sin Jesus confesses is not His own but ours, the iniquity that He has shouldered "for our sake." As St. Paul says, "For our sake [God] made Him to be sin who knew no sin" (2 Corinthians 5:21), and, "Christ redeemed us from the curse of the law by becoming a curse for us" (Galatians 3:13). In his commentary on Galations, Martin Luther explains Jesus' "confession" similarly:

> But why is Christ punished? Is it not because He has sin and bears sin? That Christ has sin is the testimony of the Holy Spirit in the Psalms. Thus in Psalm 40:12 we read, "My iniquities have overtaken Me"; in Psalm 41:4, "I said: 'O Lord, be gracious to Me; heal Me, for I have sinned against Thee!'"; and in Psalm 69:5, "O God, Thou knowest My folly; the wrongs I have done are not hidden from Thee." In these psalms the Holy Spirit is speaking in the Person of Christ and testifying in clear words that He has sinned or has sins. These testimonies of the psalms are not the words of an innocent one; they are the words of the suffering Christ, who undertook to bear the person of all sinners and therefore was made guilty of the sins of the entire world. (AE 26:279)

Therefore, these two believers, David and the divine Son of David, while persecuted, slandered, and threatened, petition their heavenly Father, voicing in unison this prayer from the psalms.

The narrative of Absalom's coup, filled with political intrigue, backstabbing, death, and restoration, provides a pattern for the history of Jesus' Passion. In both, the core question is this: Who is the divinely anointed king of Israel? David or Absalom, Jesus or Caesar? In both accounts, those former servants—Ahithophel and Judas—betray their masters, then slip a noose around their own necks. In both, the anointed king is persecuted but finally vindicated by the Lord.

Absalom: David's Enemy Son

David authored not only Psalm 41 in the context of Absalom's rebellion, but Psalm 3 was written at this time too. Read through this psalm. What does David say about his enemies? How does he describe God and what the Lord does for him? In what way does this psalm help you to interpret theologically what was going on during Absalom's coup?

As mentioned above, Psalm 41 was not the only psalm David authored during this coup of Absalom. Psalm 3 was also written during this time

period, for the superscription reads: "A Psalm of David, when he fled from Absalom his son." In this short prayer, the king bemoans how his foes have mushroomed. They taunt, "There is no salvation for him in God" (Psalm 3:2). David, however, confidently asserts that God is his shield, glory, and vindication. "From His holy hill," the Lord will hear and answer the plea of His servant (v. 4). Thus David confesses, "I lay down and slept; I woke again, for the LORD sustained me" (v. 5). Myriads of adversaries do not cause him to tremble, for the fist of the divine warrior, to whom salvation belongs, will pummel his enemies on the cheek, shattering their teeth (vv. 6–7).

Nowhere in the New Testament is this psalm expressly connected with Jesus. Yet, it is as much His prayer as David's. Indeed, inasmuch as Christ is the preeminent pray-er, one can say that the psalms are first and foremost His prayers. Just as Old Testament institutions, actions, and persons foreshadowed Him and found their perfected reality in Him, so with the psalms as well. They are perfectly prayed by Him. Furthermore, as we discovered in our discussion of Psalm 41, this historical background of Absalom's rebellion—the rebellion that prompted the composition of Psalm 3—provides a preview of what happened during the week of our Lord's Passion.

The superscription of Psalm 3 says, "When [David] fled from Absalom his son." Look back over the verses that describe David's flight (2 Samuel 15:13–37), especially focusing on David's movements in verses 23 and 30. This happened on the day in which David was betrayed by his own "Judas Iscariot." Compare David's movements with those of Jesus on the night in which He was betrayed. Read John 18:1 and Matthew 26:30. What parallels do you see between these incidents in the sufferings of David and Jesus?

As mentioned above, David prayed Psalm 3 "when he fled from Absalom his son." Having been informed that "the hearts of the men of Israel [had] gone after Absalom" (2 Samuel 15:13), David "crossed the brook Kidron" (2 Samuel 15:23) with his comrades and "went up the ascent of the Mount of Olives, weeping as he went, barefoot and with his head covered" (2 Samuel 15:30). Johann Gerhard, a Lutheran pastor and theologian from the early 1600s, observes that these unhappy actions and the places with which they are connected, prefigured what happened on the night our Lord was betrayed:

> In 2 Samuel 15, it is recorded that David, as he was fleeing from his son Absalom, left Jerusalem, crossed over the brook of Kidron and went up the Mount of Olives with weeping and sadness. This sad departure by David was a type of the departure which the Son of David, Jesus Christ, with similar sadness and trembling, would one day take across the brook Kidron [and] up the Mount of Olives as the time of His suffering finally arrived, His spoiled children running from Him for their lives. (An Explanation of the History of the Suffering and Death of our Lord Jesus Christ [Malone, TX: Repristination Press, 1999], 45–46).

Having retraced the footsteps of David, Jesus quite fittingly began to pray, even as His precursor had done in the words of the Third Psalm.

As David prayed Psalm 3 when he was betrayed by Ahithophel as well as his son Absalom, so also the words fit perfectly on the lips of our Lord on the night in which He was betrayed. Read Psalm 3 again, as if Jesus Himself were praying it. How do these words fit the context of Maundy Thursday night? Good Friday? Easter?

If the words of Psalm 3 reflect David's situation at the time of his betrayal, how much more do they mirror the night of Maundy Thursday! The adversaries of Jesus increased; many rose up against Him (Psalm 3:1). In a handful of hours, these foes would jeer that God would not deliver Him (Psalm 3:2; Matthew 27:43). Despite His suffering, however, Jesus knew that the Lord was His "shield . . . glory, and the lifter of [His] head" (Psalm 3:3).

Given the events of Good Friday and the forthcoming day of resurrection, how especially appropriate is this confession: "I lay down and slept; I woke again, for the LORD sustained Me" (Psalm 3:5) as if

to say, "I lay down in My death on Friday and slept in the tomb on the Sabbath; I woke again in My resurrection on Sunday, for the LORD sustains Me." The words of Psalm 3 become one more way through which the reader perceives how the messianic future is present in this Davidic narrative from the past.

Conclusion

Of all the men in the Old Testament whose deeds and sufferings foreshadowed those of Jesus, King David certainly ranks among the top three. In fact, so closely was he connected with the Messiah already in the Old Testament that the prophets several times give the name *David* to the Messiah Himself (Jeremiah 30:9; Ezekiel 34:23–24; 37:24–25; Hosea 3:5)! In this lesson, we have focused on the narratives from David's life in which he especially shows the ways that the Suffering Servant will face betrayal, hatred, plots, and death threats on His way to the cross. But willing and ready, He took on all that His adversaries threw at Him. He was driven by nothing less than divine love for sinners—even the sinners who personally planned and carried out deeds of evil against Him. Thanks be to God that our new and true King David, the Son of God Himself, did not shrink from the path of sufferings laid out before Him. He walked that path, all the way to Calvary and out of the tomb, out of love for us.

Prayer

Almighty and everlasting God, the consolation of the sorrowful and the strength of the weak, may the prayers of those who in any tribulation or distress cry to You graciously come before You, so that in all their necessities they may mark and receive Your manifold help and comfort; through Jesus Christ, our Lord. Amen.

(Prayer for the Afflicted and Distressed, *Lutheran Worship*, p. 126)

CHOSEN LEADER DAVID

Introduction

We often think of biblical persons in pairs, such as Adam and Eve. What are some other pairs of biblical characters that spring to mind? What names would associate most closely with David?

Take a moment to review the life of David. Perhaps in the introduction to a study Bible you can find a survey of the events in **1–2 Samuel**, the books that document David's deeds and misdeeds. Acquaint yourself with the major events in his life.

Not only was David a king and warrior, he was also a poet. Look through the Book of Psalms and notice how many times David's name appears in the heading of the psalm. What else is sometimes described in these headings? See, for instance, **Psalms 3**; **18**; **51**; **56**; and **59**. What profit might there be in reading these psalms alongside the historical events that gave rise to them? What might they show us?

"Saul, Saul, Why Do You Persecute Me?" David and Saul

Saul was the first king of Israel. Though he began his reign well, things soon went sour. Read through **1 Samuel 13:1–15** and **1 Samuel 15** for examples of his wrongdoing. Note especially **15:28**. What does the prophet Samuel tell Saul the Lord will do? How do you suppose this affected Saul? What would he begin to do?

David was secretly anointed king in 1 Samuel 16, but, of course, Saul was unaware of this. Trace the events through which Saul became acquainted with David? You'll find these in **1 Samuel 16:14–18:5**. In this initial stage, what did Saul think of David? How would you characterize their relationship?

It wasn't long before Saul began to realize that David was the "neighbor" whom Samuel said would replace Saul (**15:28**). Read **1 Samuel 18:6–9**. What sparked the friction between the two men? What emotions were driving Saul?

A Window of Escape

The rest of **1 Samuel** describes the many and various way in which Saul persecuted David. We will only examine a couple of them. The first deals with David's family. Read the following verses to understand how closely knit David was to the family of Saul: **1 Samuel 18:1–4** and **18:17–30**. What kind of relationships did he have with Saul's children?

Our story is found in **1 Samuel 19:11–18**. As background to Saul's murderous actions, read **1 Samuel 18:10–11**; **18:25**; **19:1**;

and **19:10**. Through what efforts had Saul already tried to send David to an early grave?

Read **1 Samuel 19:11–18**. Describe the actions and attitudes of the various characters in the story. How does this account highlight the determination of Saul to murder his rival?

You might wonder what was going through David's mind on this night of danger and escape. Some of these questions are answered by reading **Psalm 59**. Note the superscription of the psalm. As you read through the psalm, describe how David interprets this event. What are the key themes in this psalm? How does David speak of God and his enemies? What does he expect the Lord to be and to do for him?

Consider the connection this event in David's life has to the life of Jesus. To aid you, read through the psalm again, this time thinking of Christ as the one who prays these words. How do they fit with the life and sufferings of our Lord? How are David's words just as fitting—indeed, even more so—on the lips of Jesus?

Consider also the historic incident behind this psalm in the light of what happened to Jesus. Relate the actions of David's enemies to what the enemies of Jesus did to Him in these verses: **Mark 3:2**; **Luke 14:1**; **20:20**; **John 5:18**; **7:1**; **11:53**. The Lord rescued David; how did Christ similarly escape from His foes? See **John 8:59** and **11:54**.

David the Madman

The next incident is admittedly a rather bizarre one. Read **1 Samuel 21:10–15**. Bearing in mind that Gath was a city filled with David's enemies, the Philistines, how might they interpret his actions? Why did he do what he did? What was the result?

David also composed a song or prayer after this incident: **Psalm 34**. Read through the psalm. What is the main message of this prayer? What are some of its primary themes?

Keeping in mind **Psalm 34:20**, read **John 19:31–37**. In **19:36**, John says these things happened to fulfill the Scriptures. To which Scriptures is John referring? In **19:36**, John likely has two verses in mind: **Exodus 12:46** and **Psalm 34:20**. What is the Exodus passage about? What connection does the New Testament draw between the Passover lamb and Jesus? See **John 1:36** and **1 Corinthians 5:7**. Compare also the verse in the psalm with what happened to Jesus on the cross. How does this fit both the suffering of David in Gath and the suffering of Jesus on the cross? Read **Psalm 34** anew, in light of the crucifixion of Jesus. How does this open up a new understanding of the psalm? Which words seem especially appropriate when heard as prayed by our Savior?

David Betrayed

David's sufferings did not end when he finally assumed the throne as king of Israel (**2 Samuel 2:1–4** and **5:1–5**). In many ways they increased! Survey the events narrated in 2 Samuel. What were some of the lowest points in David's reign? With which group of people did most of his sufferings originate?

Ahithophel: David's "Judas Iscariot"

The events we're about to study took place during Absalom's rebellion. To acquaint yourself with Absalom and his past, skim **2 Samuel 13–18**. Answer the following: Who was Absalom in relation to David? Why did Absalom have to flee Jerusalem? What did he do when he returned? What evil did he perpetrate against the king? How did he die?

One of the men who rebelled against David during Absalom's coup was Ahithophel. How highly esteemed was this counselor of David (**2 Samuel 16:23**)? What did he do when Absalom asked him to join in the rebellion (**2 Samuel**

15:12)? What did David pray concerning Ahithophel (**2 Samuel 15:31**)?

Absalom asked advice from two men: Ahithophel and Hushai. What counsel did Ahithophel give (**2 Samuel 17:1–4**)? Given his past record (**2 Samuel 16:23**), what reaction did he likely expect when he urged the leader to do such and such? What counsel did Hushai give (**2 Samuel 17:5–14**)? Whose advice did Absalom follow? Why did it turn out this way?

How did Ahithophel respond to the rejection of his counsel (**2 Samuel 17:23**)? Why? What drove him to do this?

Although there is no superscription in **Psalm 41** that confirms it was written during Absalom's rebellion, the content strongly suggests it was. Read through the psalm. How did David's adversaries treat him? How does David respond? What in particular does David say about his enemy in **Psalm 41:9**?

How is Ahithophel like Judas Iscariot, who betrayed Jesus? In what kind of relationship did each stand with his leader? What did each do to sell out his master? Moreover, compare how the two men ended their lives. Read **2 Samuel 17:23** with **Matthew 27:5**.

Read **John 13:18–19**. What is the context in which Jesus says these words? What psalm does He quote? Note that as David prays this with Ahithophel in mind, Jesus prays it with Judas in mind.

How does the rest of **Psalm 41** fit the life and sufferings of both David and the Son of David? Note that in **Psalm 41:4**,

David confesses his own sin. If this prayer is prayed by the Messiah, how could He confess sins? Answer this question in light of **2 Corinthians 5:21** and **Galatians 3:13**. Whose sin is Jesus actually confessing?

Absalom: David's Enemy Son

David authored not only **Psalm 41** in the context of Absalom's rebellion, but Psalm 3 was written at this time too. Read through this psalm. What does David say about his enemies? How does he describe God and what the Lord does for him? In what way does this psalm help you to interpret theologically what was going on during Absalom's coup?

The superscription of **Psalm 3** says, "When [David] fled from Absalom his son." Look back over the verses that describe David's flight (**2 Samuel 15:13–37**), especially focusing on David's movements in **verses 23** and **30**. This happened on the day in which David was betrayed by his own "Judas Iscariot." Compare David's movements with those of Jesus on the night in which He was betrayed. Read **John 18:1** and **Matthew 26:30**. What parallels do you see between these incidents in the sufferings of David and Jesus?

As David prayed **Psalm 3** when he was betrayed by Ahithophel as well as his son Absalom, so also the words fit perfectly on the lips of our Lord, on the night in which He was betrayed. Read **Psalm 3** again, as if Jesus Himself were praying it. How do these words fit the context of Maundy Thursday night? Good Friday? Easter?

PERSECUTOR AND PREACHER PAUL

Prayer

Almighty God, You turned the heart of him who persecuted the Church and by his preaching caused the light of the Gospel to shine throughout the world. Grant us ever to rejoice in the saving light of Your Gospel and, following the example of the apostle Paul, to spread it to the ends of the earth; through Jesus Christ, who lives and reigns with You and the Holy Spirit, one God, now and forever. Amen.

(Collect for the Conversion of Saint Paul, *Lutheran Service Book*)

Paul: A Man of Many Names and Many Sufferings

What are some names and titles that we often associate with Paul? How does each of these shed light on his person and office?

We know him by many names and titles: Saul and Paul, persecutor and preacher, apostle and evangelist, pastor and missionary, saint and—by his own admission—chief of sinners (1 Timothy 1:15). At one time or another in his famous life, each of these titles fit the man and his deeds.

Before Paul was an apostle of the Church, he was a persecutor of Christianity. Read through the following verses to see what he did to try to stamp out the faith: Acts 7:54–60; 8:3; 9:1–2; 22:4. What happened to change the course of Paul's life? See Acts 9:1–19. What does Christ say with regard to Paul and sufferings in 9:16?

In the earliest days of the Christian Church, Saul became one of the archenemies of the followers of Jesus. His own testimony says, "I persecuted this Way [Christianity] to the death, binding and delivering to prison both men and women, as the high priest and the whole counsel of elders can bear me witness" (Acts 22:4–5). He witnessed and approved the stoning of Stephen, the first Christian martyr (Acts 7:54–60). Saul spent his days "ravaging the church, and entering house after house, he dragged off men and women and committed them to prison" (Acts 8:3). While Paul was "still breathing threats and murder against the disciples of the Lord," he obtained official letters from the high priest to travel to Damascus that he might bring Christians bound to Jerusalem for punishment (Acts 9:1–2). While on this journey to Damascus, Christ appeared and spoke to Saul, bringing him to repentance and calling

him to be His "chosen instrument" to carry the truth of the Gospel "before the Gentiles and kings and the children of Israel" (Acts 9:15).

Paul has much to say about suffering and the Christian life. Read through the following verses, and summarize some of Paul's main points regarding what it means to bear the cross: Philippians 1:29; 3:10; 2 Corinthians 1:5; Romans 8:18; Colossians 1:24. In this last verse, Paul says he is "filling up what is lacking in Christ's afflictions." Was something truly "lacking" in the sufferings of Jesus? What does Paul mean?

These last words were spoken by God to Ananias, the man chosen to preach to Saul and baptize him in Damascus. The Lord also added, "I will show him how much he must suffer for the sake of My name" (Acts 9:16). And suffer he did! These words appear to be packed with foreboding, like a black cloud hanging on the horizon, threatening a terrorizing storm . . . so it seems to us. But Paul chose not to view his future life this way. Indeed, Paul suffered much, but his attitude toward this suf-

fering was far different from what we might expect. Though Paul certainly did not welcome suffering with a foolish grin on his face, he did embrace it faithfully as part of the believer's lot in this fallen world. Paul viewed sufferings as the way in which our lives are conformed to the life of the crucified Christ. He wrote to the church in Philippi, for instance, that he wished to "share [Christ's] sufferings, becoming like Him in His death, that by any means possible [he] might attain the resurrection from the dead" (Philippians 3:10). Paul also told these Christians that "it has been granted to you that for the sake of Christ you should not only believe in Him but also suffer for His sake." (Philippians 1:29). Thus faith and suffering go hand in glove; the first always entails the second. With such suffering, however, also comes consolation. As Paul told the Christians in Corinth, "For as we share abundantly in Christ's sufferings, so through Christ we share abundantly in comfort too" (2 Corinthians 1:5).

By far the most incredible statement from the apostle Paul regarding suffering is what he told the

Christians in Colossae: "Now I rejoice in my sufferings for your sake, and in my flesh I am filling up what is lacking in Christ's afflictions for the sake of His body, that is, the church" (Colossians 1:24). Now what could Paul mean when he says he is "filling up what is lacking in Christ's afflictions"? Is he implying that Jesus did not suffer enough? Are Paul's crosses somehow completing our salvation? No, definitely not. That is not what Paul is saying. The sufferings of Jesus were, of course, fully sufficient for our salvation. Nothing remains to be done. As Jesus cried out from the cross, "It is finished" (John 19:30).

But the sufferings of the members of Christ's body, the Church, are not over. As Luther says in a comment on Paul's words, "It is as if [St. Paul] were saying: His whole Christendom is not fully completed; we too must follow after, in order that none of the sufferings of Christ may be lacking or lost, but all brought together into one. Therefore every Christian must be aware that sufferings will not fail to come" (AE 51:198).

In this closing session, we will take a close look at how Paul's sufferings in particular were "filling up what is lacking in Christ's afflictions." We shall see what Paul has in common with sufferings servants such as Joseph, Moses, Job, and David—that his life and ministry were a reflection of the ministry of the Suffering Servant.

A Catalog of Sufferings

Before looking at particular events in Paul's ministry in which he suffered for the sake of the Gospel, read through the following passages that summarize the main trials Paul faced: 2 Corinthians 6:3–10; 11:23–29. Why did Paul face so many dangers? Who were his enemies? What is the tone of these lists, that is, what message is Paul communicating? Why would he find it helpful or necessary to remind the church in Corinth of his perils and afflictions?

Before we look at specific incidents in Paul's life, first survey a couple of sections in his Epistles where he provides what one might call a catalog of sufferings. These lists bear witness not only to the

crosses borne by preachers such as Paul, but they also declare the fidelity of the apostle, who remained steadfast in his work despite the fact that he faced such seemingly insurmountable obstacles.

Both of the catalogs we'll look at are in St. Paul's Second Letter to the church in Corinth. The apostle had good reasons for reminding the Corinthians—as opposed to some other congregation—of all that he had suffered in the Office of the Holy Ministry. The Christians in Corinth, it appears, were under the influence of false teachers in their midst who disparaged the ministry of Paul (2 Corinthians 10–11). He chides his hearers for putting up with those who preach "another Jesus," another Spirit, another Gospel than the one that Paul proclaimed (2 Corinthians 11:4). He mocks these teachers as "super-apostles" who in reality are "false apostles, deceitful workmen" who disguise "themselves as apostles of Christ" (2 Corinthians 11:5, 13). Thus, in his Letter to the Corinthians, one of Paul's goals is to remind the people of his apostolic authority, his unselfish ministry to them, and—as one testimony to the truthfulness of his office—all he has suffered for the name of Christ.

In the first of these catalogs, St. Paul says,

We put no obstacle in anyone's way, so that no fault may be found with our ministry, but as servants of God we commend ourselves in every way: by great endurance, in afflictions, hardships, calamities, beatings, imprisonments, riots, labors, sleepless nights, hunger; by purity, knowledge, patience, kindness, the Holy Spirit, genuine love; by truthful speech, and the power of God; with the weapons of righteousness for the right hand and for the left; through honor and dishonor, through slander and praise. We are treated as imposters, and yet are true; as unknown, and yet well known; as dying, and behold, we live; as punished, and yet not killed; as sorrowful, yet always rejoicing; as poor, yet making many rich; as having nothing, yet possessing everything. (2 Corinthians 6:3–10)

The second list is like the first, yet even more specific with regard to the kinds of sufferings endured by Paul. Contrasting himself with the "false apostles" (2 Corinthians 11:13), Paul says he has

Far greater labors, far more imprisonments, with

countless beatings, and often near death. Five times I received at the hands of the Jews the forty lashes less one. Three times I was beaten with rods. Once I was stoned. Three times I was shipwrecked; a night and a day I was adrift at sea; on frequent journeys, in dangers from rivers, danger from robbers, danger from my own people, danger from Gentiles, danger in the city, danger in the wilderness, danger at sea, danger from false brothers; in toil and hardship, through many a sleepless night, in hunger and thirst, often without food, in cold and exposure. And, apart from other things, there is the daily pressure on me of my anxiety for all the churches. Who is weak, and I am not weak? Who is made to fall, and I am not indignant? (2 Corinthians 11:23–29)

Needless to say, for the apostle Paul, suffering became a way of life, for his way of life was the way of the cross. He faced pains of deprivation (hunger, thirst, cold), pains of punishment (beatings, lashings, imprisonments), pains of heart (slander, anxiety for the churches, false brothers), and countless others kinds of afflictions. Such was the life of preaching the crucified Christ; it, too, was a life of crucifixion, but it was one that led in the end to resurrection and life everlasting.

Arrested and Jailed at Philippi

We'll first look at what happened to Paul during his stay in Philippi. During Paul's missionary journeys, what did he typically do when he entered a city? See Acts 13:5; 13:13–15, 43; and 14:1. Why would Paul preach in these places? Why should the hearers have already been ready for Paul's message?

After the conversion of Paul, he began "preaching the faith he once tried to destroy" (Galatians 1:23). On more than one mission trip, Paul proclaimed the advent, sacrifice, and resurrection of the Messiah to all who would hear his message—and many who would not! Numerous cities established congregations and appointed pastors so that as Paul moved on, the message of the Gospel would continue to be proclaimed and the Sacraments celebrated. These journeys, however, were fraught with difficulties and persecutions from both Jews and Gentiles

who opposed the Christian proclamation. One of the most memorable of these occurred in the city of Philippi.

Read Acts 16:11–15. Where did Paul go when he entered Philippi? What does this probably tell us about the Jewish population of the city? What happened when Paul preached?

On his second missionary journey, Paul and two companions—Silas and Timothy—entered Philippi (Acts 16:11–15). On the Sabbath, they found a group of worshipers who came together to pray by a river. Evidently, there was no synagogue in the city, or Paul would have preached there, as was his custom (Acts 13:5; 13:13–15, 43; 14:1). To those gathered, Paul preached the Gospel. One of those who believed his message, a woman named Lydia, opened her home to Paul and his fellow travelers.

Read Acts 16:16–24. What led to trouble for Paul? What was done to him? Had Paul and Silas done anything wrong? How do Paul and Silas exemplify what Peter talks about in 1 Peter 2:19–25?

Read Acts 16:25. What did Paul and Silas do during the night? What was the likely message of these hymns? Relate this singing of hymns to the purpose of hymns in the Church today? Why do we sing what we sing? What message should hymns convey?

Read Acts 16:26–40. Summarize the events in this chapter. Highlight the ways in which you can see God at work through His Word and Sacrament.

Trouble began soon, however, when the apostle became "greatly annoyed" at a slave girl who was possessed by a spirit of divination (2 Corinthians 16:16–24). She followed Paul and his friends for many days crying out, "These men are servants of the Most High God, who proclaim to you the way of salvation" (2 Corinthians 16:17). Finally, harassed enough, Paul said to the spirit, "I command you in the name of Jesus Christ to come out of her" (2 Corinthians 16:18). And out it came. While this was well and good for the girl, there was one snag: her owners had been making big bucks by using her for fortune-telling. When the spirit exited, their profit did as well. Irate, the men "seized Paul and Silas and dragged them into the marketplace before the rulers" (2 Corinthians 16:19). The apostle and his companion were convicted on trumped-up charges, stripped, beaten with rods, and thrown into prison.

Thanks be to God that the account goes on to end on a very bright note. Readers can get all the details in Acts 16:25–40. The long and short of the story is that, during the night, the Lord rescued Paul and Silas from prison by means of an earthquake. They preached the Gospel to the jailer and his family, and all were baptized. The next day, Paul and Silas received a personal apology and escort out of the city by the magistrates, who had unlawfully punished them, since Paul and Silas were Roman citizens.

What does Jesus say of the cross in Luke 9:23? Which crosses was Paul called to bear in Philippi? If you could pinpoint the one reason Paul was opposed in this city—and many others—what would it be?

Jesus said that a servant is not greater than his master (John 13:16). Paul, the servant, would face the same obstacles and opposition that Jesus, his Master, had faced. Read John 15:18–20. How will the world receive the messengers of Jesus? Why? It is still the same today? In what sorts of ways does the world show its hatred of the Gospel?

Some time later, Paul wrote one of his most—if not *the* most—joyful Letters and sent it to the congregation in Philippi. Among other things, he expresses in that Epistle his heartfelt wish that he "may know [Christ] and the power of His resurrection, and may share His sufferings, becoming like Him in His death, that by any means possible [he] may attain the resurrection from the dead" (Philippians 3:10–11). Paul's prayer that he might "share [Christ's] sufferings," was already answered in part during his stay in Philippi.

Jesus said that "a servant is not greater than his master" (John 13:16). He calls His every servant,

His every disciple, to "take up his cross daily and follow Me" (Luke 9:23). The crosses that Paul was called upon to bear were numerous and heavy. Paul bore them daily and indeed hourly! In Philippi, these crosses took the form of persecution, slander, injustice, beatings, and imprisonment. In the end, all of these sufferings stemmed from one source: opposition to the preaching of Paul. In this way, Paul, the servant, was certainly no greater than his Master. Indeed, even worse sufferings were inflicted upon our Lord for the very same reason.

Not only the disciples of Jesus but also preachers in the Old Testament faced opposition to the Word of God. For instance, see 1 Kings 19:1–3; Jeremiah 20:1–6; 26:1–15; 37:11–38:6; and Amos 7:10–17. What happened to these Old Testament preachers? How is the preaching of the Word opposed today? If not through outright persecution, in what other ways?

On many occasions, Jesus forewarned His disciples that the world would receive them in the same way that it had received Jesus when He proclaimed the words of His heavenly Father. For instance, Jesus told His disciples,

> If the world hates you, know that it has hated Me before it hated you. If you were of the world, the world would love you as its own; but because you are not of the world, but I chose you out of the world, therefore the world hates you. Remember the word that I said to you: "A servant is not greater than his master." If they persecuted Me, they will also persecute you. If they kept My word, they will also keep yours. (John 15:18–20)

The history of God's chosen people continues to prove this point. The brothers of Joseph hated him because of the divine word he preached to them about his dreams (Genesis 37:1–11). Moses was despised by many in Israel because of the message he proclaimed. The prophets Elijah (1 Kings 19:1–3), Jeremiah (20:1–6; 26:1–15; 37:11–38:6), Amos (7:10–17), and countless other preachers faced similar opposition from those to whom they were sent. But opposed or not, such men fulfilled their calling, as did Paul in Philippi.

It should have come as no surprise that the preaching of the Messiah would be opposed. Read Isaiah 49:1–4. This is the Messiah speaking. What language does He use to describe His labor? Why did this not stop Christ from preaching? Why do preachers still proclaim the Word today, even if they face persecution?

As we read the stories of the suffering servants of the Lord—both those who ministered before the birth of Jesus and those who, like Paul, ministered after the incarnation—we are constantly reminded of our Suffering Servant, whose preaching was also despised, as was foretold by the prophet Isaiah. In one of the Servant Songs, in which the Messiah speaks in first person, He says,

Listen to Me, O coastlands, and give attention, you peoples from afar. The LORD called Me from the womb, from the body of My mother He named My name. He made My mouth like a sharp sword; in the shadow of His hand He hid Me; He made Me a polished arrow; in His quiver He hid Me away. And He said to Me, "You are My servant, Israel, in whom I will be glorified." But I said, "I have labored in vain; I have spent My strength for nothing and vanity; yet surely My right is with the LORD, and My recompense with My God." (Isaiah 49:1–4).

The Messiah's complaint voices His frustration: "I have labored in vain; I have spent My strength for nothing and vanity." So it often seemed, for instance, as the fickle crowds one minute wanted to make Him king (John 6:15) and the next minute turned their back on Him and His Word (John 6:66). Yet Christ continued to preach, for He confessed that His "right is with the LORD, and [His] recompense with [His] God."

Despite opposition to His preaching, Christ does not zip shut the lips of heaven. He keeps right on proclaiming His message of life through His servants. Even while chained in a dungeon, Paul and Silas sang hymns that doubtlessly told about the compassion of God. No chains could shackle the Word of God! As Paul himself would later write to Timothy, "Remember Jesus Christ, risen from the dead, the offspring of David, as preached in my

gospel, for which I am suffering, bound with chains as a criminal. But the word of God is not bound!" (2 Timothy 2:8–9). This unbound Word is the message that truly frees us. It sets us free from sin and everlasting death so that we, along with the jailer and his family in Philippi, may rejoice over the grace of our Lord Jesus Christ.

Temple Trouble

On his return from a missionary trip, Paul decided to go to Jerusalem. Why did some urge him not to travel to that city? Read Acts 21:7–14. What was Paul's response?

On his return from a missionary trip, Paul made up his mind to journey to Jerusalem. Though strongly urged not to travel there for fear of the persecution and possible death he would endure at the hands of the Jews (Acts 21:7–14), Paul was adamant. He testified, "I am ready not only to be imprisoned but even to die in Jerusalem for the name of the Lord Jesus" (Acts 21:13). And die he almost did.

When Paul arrived in Jerusalem, he spent some time in the temple. Read Acts 21:27–36. What happened one day while he was there? Why did the false charge against him anger the crowd so much?

What was Paul allowed to do? Read Acts 21:40–22:21. Paul preached to a crowd ready to tear him apart! What does this tell us about the man?

Upon Paul's arrival, all went well for the first few days. Later, however, when he entered the temple, some of his Jewish enemies from Asia, who were in Jerusalem for the festival of Pentecost (20:16; 21:27), recognized Paul and stirred up the crowd against him. They cried out, "Men of Israel, help! This is the man who is teaching everyone everywhere against the people and the law and this place. Moreover, he even brought Greeks into the temple and has defiled this holy place" (Acts 21:28). Though the charges were patently false, it made no difference. "All the city was stirred up, and the people ran together. They seized Paul and dragged him out of the temple, and at once the gates were shut" (Acts 21:30). The apostle would soon have been beaten to death by the bloodthirsty mob had not a band of Roman soldiers stopped them and arrested Paul. The rabble was so enraged that Paul had to be carried by the soldiers to keep him above their murderous hands (Acts 21:35). After a few minutes, Paul was allowed to address the crowd and even to preach the Gospel (Acts 21:40–22:21). But the second he mentioned the fact that the Lord had sent him to the Gentiles (22:21), the crowd of Jews once more grew hot with rage. It was vain to continue.

The next few chapters describe Paul's long time in chains, his many trials, and his eventual in-house imprisonment in Rome. Read Acts 28:30–31. How did Paul use his time in Rome?

Thus began Paul's extended imprisonment by the Romans. He would spend month after month appearing before councils and judges, narrowly escaping the murderous plots of his adversaries, suffering shipwreck, in chains and behind bars from Jerusalem to Rome. Along the way, at every opportunity, Paul would not fail to proclaim the message of the crucified Christ. Even while under house imprisonment in Rome, for two years, Paul "welcomed all who came to him, proclaiming the kingdom of God and teaching about the Lord Jesus Christ with all boldness and without hindrance" (Acts 28:30–31).

The persecution of Paul this time began in the temple. Beginning already in the Old Testament, godly preachers faced hatred, rejection, and even death in the temple courts. For instance, what happened to Zechariah in the temple? Read 2 Chronicles 24:20–22. On many occasions, like Paul, Jesus also faced hostile forces in the temple. Read through the following texts: Matthew 21:12–17, 23–27; John 7:32–44; 10:39. What made the temple such a dangerous place for Christ and His preachers?

Early Christian preachers, such as Paul, continued Jesus' practice of teaching in the temple—a practice that caused more than a little trouble for many of them. In His ministry, Jesus often encountered opposition there. He drove the moneychangers from the temple (Matthew 21:12–17), faced there the hostile questions of the chief priests and elders (Matthew 21:23–27), and more than once was nearly arrested for teaching in the temple courts (John 7:32–44; 10:39). After Jesus' ascension, Peter and John preached the Gospel in the area of the temple called "Solomon's portico" (Acts 3:11). They were arrested, tried, and sternly warned "not to speak or teach at all in the name of Jesus" (Acts 4:18; see also vv. 1–17), a warning they steadfastly refused to obey. The violence directed at Paul for his proclamation in the temple was thus right in line with what had transpired there before. Indeed, in the Old Testament as well, prophets such as Jeremiah (Jeremiah 7:2–4) and Zechariah (2 Chronicles 24:20–22) preached the divine Word in the vicinity of the temple. In the case of Zechariah, this preaching led to martyrdom in the very courts of the Lord's house!

Despite the dangers of preaching at the temple, what also made it an ideal place for the proclamation of the Good News of the Messiah's arrival? Review the following texts to see the relation of the temple, its priests, and its sacrifices to the Messiah: Matthew 12:6; John 1:14; 2:19–21; Hebrews 7:11–28; 9:11–14.

What was it about the temple that led to such (often violent) confrontations? The chief reason was that the temple was "home turf" for religious authorities—men who were often the target of chastisement by the preacher for their wrongdoing. They did not like being called to account in the very place where they thought they were supposed to be in charge. So, more often than not, they reacted angrily, even murderously, when the message called them to repentance. In the case of Paul, we see that it was not merely the bigwigs who were after him, but the general populace as well (Acts 21:30).

Though full of dangers for the Christian preacher, the temple was still an ideal place for the proclamation of the Gospel. One reason was that it served as the center of Jewish religious rites. Though pious Jews attended synagogue services every Sabbath and other times as well, many made annual or multi-annual pilgrimages to Jerusalem on the festivals of Passover, Pentecost, or Tabernacles to worship at the temple. Since these faithful worshipers awaited the coming of the Messiah, it was the perfect place to proclaim that He had already come.

Second, the message of the Gospel is intimately joined with the ultimate purpose of the temple. Both the Old Testament tabernacle and temple were where God dwelt among sinners, where priests ministered, where sacrifices were offered. The Good News preached by Jesus, as well as Peter and Paul, was that One greater than the temple had arrived (Matthew 12:6). He is the "Word [who] became flesh and dwelt [literally, "tabernacled"] among us" (John 1:14). He told the Jews, "Destroy this temple, and in three days I will raise it up" (John 2:19). Yet the "temple" of which He spoke was His body (John 2:21). In addition, Christ came as the "great high priest" (Hebrews 4:14) who perfectly fulfilled the priesthood only foreshadowed by the Levites (Hebrews 7:11–28). Moreover, Christ was the complete, perfect, "once for all" sacrifice that brought an end to the old covenant and the animal sacrifices (Hebrews 9:11–14). Therefore, the Gospel so often preached at the temple said, "This temple, these priests, these sacrifices are obsolete! For He who is the perfect Temple, perfect Priest, and perfect Sacrifice has come." No wonder the authorities—for whom the temple was their bread and butter—became so angry when Christians preachers used the temple precincts as their public pulpit!

Reflect back on what you have studied about Paul, his conversion, his sufferings, and the way in which the Lord sustained him. How was Paul—like Joseph, Job, Moses, and David—also an "image of God's Son"?

Paul's preaching and suffering at the temple was thus in synch with what Jesus had done before him. One of the ways he shared "abundantly in Christ's sufferings" (2 Corinthians 1:5) was by imitation of Him: preaching where He preached, suffering

at the very hands of those who earlier arrested and crucified the Lord Jesus.

Conclusion

Like Joseph, Moses, Job, David, and many others, so Paul, too, serves as an "image of God's Son"—one in whose life we see the Christ at work to show forth His own life. Whether singing the Gospel in the Philippian jail or preaching the Gospel while surrounded by his would-be murderers, Paul was always about the work of the Crucified One. Jesus delivered on His promise to show this once persecutor turned apostle "how much he must suffer for the sake of [Christ's] name" (Acts 9:16). But suffer what he may, Paul knew and confessed that "the sufferings of this present time are not worth comparing with the glory that is to be revealed to us" (Romans 8:18). Paul now shares that glory with the Church triumphant, the saints in heaven who surround the throne of God and of the Lamb (Revelation 7:9–10).

We, too, who believe in the same Christ that Paul preached, eagerly await the day when we shall leave this valley of suffering to inherit the glory prepared for us since the foundation of the world. May God's Son, the Suffering Servant, keep us ever in His grace that we may join Paul and all those who once suffered on earth who now enjoy the bliss of life in the heavenly Fatherland.

Closing Prayer

Almighty and everlasting God, You sent Your Son, our Savior Jesus Christ, to take upon Himself our flesh and suffer death upon the cross. Mercifully grant that we may follow the example of His great humility and patience and be made partakers of His resurrection; through the same Jesus Christ, our Lord, who lives and reigns with You and the Holy Spirit, one God, now and forever. Amen.

(Collect for Palm Sunday, *Lutheran Service Book*)

PERSECUTOR AND PREACHER PAUL

Paul: A Man of Many Names and Many Sufferings

What are some names and titles that we often associate with Paul? How does each of these shed light on his person and office?

Before Paul was an apostle of the Church, he was a persecutor of Christianity. Read through the following verses to see what he did to try to stamp out the faith: **Acts 7:54–60**; **8:3**; **9:1–2**; **22:4**. What happened to change the course of Paul's life? See **Acts 9:1–19**. What does Christ say with regard to Paul and sufferings in **9:16**?

Paul has much to say about suffering and the Christian life. Read through the following verses, and summarize some of Paul's main points regarding what it means to bear the cross: **Philippians 1:29**; **3:10**; **2 Corinthians 1:5**; **Romans 8:18**; **Colossians 1:24**. In this last verse, Paul says he is "filling up what is lacking in Christ's afflictions." Was something truly "lacking" in the sufferings of Jesus? What does Paul mean?

A Catalog of Sufferings

Before looking at particular events in Paul's ministry in which he suffered for the sake of the Gospel, read through the following passages that summarize the main trials Paul faced: **2 Corinthians 6:3–10**; **11:23–29**. Why did Paul face so many dangers? Who were his enemies? What is the tone of these lists, that is, what message is Paul communicating? Why would he find it helpful or necessary to remind the church in Corinth of his perils and afflictions?

Arrested and Jailed at Philippi

We'll first look at what happened to Paul during his stay in Philippi. During Paul's missionary journeys, what did he typically do when he entered a city? See **Acts 13:5**, **13:13–14**, **43**; and **14:1**. Why would Paul preach in these places? Why should the hearers have already been ready for Paul's message?

Read **Acts 16:11–15**. Where did Paul go when he entered Philippi? What does this probably tell us about the Jewish population of the city? What happened when Paul preached?